Good Housekeeping
FREEZER
HANDBOOK

Good Housekeeping

FREEZER
HANDBOOK

EBURY PRESS
LONDON

This edition published 1995

First published in 1991
by Ebury Press, Random House, 20 Vauxhall Bridge Road,
London SW1V 2SA

7 9 10 8 6

Random House Australia Pty Limited, 20 Alfred Street, Milsons Point,
Sydney, New South Wales 2061, Australia

Random House New Zealand Limited, 18 Poland Road, Glenfield,
Auckland 10, New Zealand

Random House South Africa Pty Limited, PO Box 337, Bergvlei,
South Africa

Random House UK Limited Reg. No. 954009

A CIP catalogue record for this book is available from the
British Library.

ISBN 0 712647139

Editor: Barbara Croxford
Designer: Roger Daniels
Photographer: Ferguson Hill
Stylist: Ian Hands
Home Economist: Allyson Birch

Typeset by Textype Typesetters, Cambridge
Printed and bound in Great Britain by BPC Hazel Books Ltd,
Aylesbury, Buckinghamshire

CONTENTS

INTRODUCTION

Owning a freezer means you can shop less often, cook only when you feel like it, preserve produce straight from the garden (and any you might buy cheaply at the height of the season) and you will always have meals at the ready for unexpected occasions.

Freezing retains more of the quality, character and nutritive value of the food than other preserving methods, and takes only a fraction of the time that curing, smoking, pickling and bottling take.

A freezer will mean different things to different people, but to all it will give added convenience. The type and size will depend on the usage and number of people in the household. For example, to a working mother it will mean less lunch hour shopping. To the keen gardener, surplus produce can be frozen for use later in the year. For the elderly, it would cut out shopping when tired or in bad weather. And for those who frequently entertain, it will enable batch cooking, saving time, effort and money.

TWENTY FREEZING TIPS

1 Freeze only good quality foods. A freezer cannot work miracles; what comes out is only as good as what went in.

2 Handle food as little as possible and keep everything scrupulously clean. Freezing doesn't kill bacteria or germs.

3 Pack and seal food carefully. Food that is exposed to air or moisture will deteriorate and there is a risk of cross flavouring or transfer of smells from food that is inadequately wrapped.

4 Never put anything hot or even warm into a freezer. It will raise the temperature of other items in there and possibly cause deterioration. Cool food rapidly once it has been cooked or blanched either by plunging vegetables in a bowl of iced water or by standing the dish in a bowl of iced water.

5 Freeze food as quickly as possible so that it retains its texture, colour, taste and nutritional value.

6 Pack food in small quantities. It will thaw more quickly and you can get out more than one pack if necessary.

7 Follow the manufacturer's instructions on use of the fast-freeze switch and where in the cabinet to freeze down food.

8 Don't pack food that is to be frozen too closely together. Spread it out until frozen.

9 Move newly-frozen items from the fast-freeze area once they are frozen.

10 Remember to switch the fast-freeze control back to the normal setting once food has been frozen.

11 Do not keep opening the door of your freezer; it raises the temperature inside the cabinet. Decide what you want to get out and remove it quickly.

12 Use a freezer thermometer to help you to maintain a steady storage temperature of $-18°C$ ($0°F$). Move it around within the freezer to check that the temperature is maintained throughout the cabinet.

13 Label and date food so that you can rotate stock efficiently. Consider keeping a freezer log book to stop you going through the contents to see what you have stored.

14 Defrost the freezer when stocks are low and preferably on a cold day. Do the job as fast as you can so that the contents can be put back into the freezer as quickly as possible.

15 Tape the address of the service organisation to an inconspicuous spot on the freezer casing or inside the adjacent kitchen cupboard door.

16 Know what to do in emergencies, such as a power cut or freezer breakdown.

17 If you are storing a large quantity of food, particularly expensive items, consider taking out special freezer insurance to cover you against loss.

18 If your freezer is in a garage or outhouse, fit a freezer alarm to it so that you have immediate warning if anything goes wrong, and fit a lock.

19 Put a plug with a built-in alarm on the freezer to warn you if the fuse blows.

20 Keep your freezer full to keep running costs down. Fill gaps with basics like bread or, if you are running down your stock to defrost, fill the gaps with old towels or crumpled newspaper.

WHAT NOT TO FREEZE

Although some foods can be frozen in one form or another, there are some items that just lose all their eating appeal if you freeze them. Here is a list of what doesn't work well.

Bananas turn black. This can be improved if the flesh is mashed with lemon juice and used in a recipe.

Caviar tends to go rather watery.

Cheese Full fat soft cheese can only be frozen if it contains at least 40 per cent butterfat. Cottage, curd and low fat soft cheeses do not freeze well, though they can be frozen in cooked dishes. Hard cheeses freeze satisfactorily, but the longer they remain in the freezer the more crumbly they become. Blue cheese becomes crumbly when frozen but can be used for cooking.

Egg custard separates out. However, canned custard freezes satisfactorily.

Eggs cannot to be frozen in the shell and when hard-boiled they become tough and watery and the white turns grey. Egg whites and whole beaten eggs freeze well, but separated yolks become gummy unless salt or sugar is added.

Gelatine Do not freeze dishes containing a very high proportion of gelatine, especially anything depending entirely on it as the stabilising agent, for example a moulded jelly. Gelatine-based recipes like soufflés and mousses freeze well for up to about one month.

Hollandaise sauce, mayonnaise and other egg-based sauces tend to separate.

Jam used in large amounts or as a filling has a tendency to liquefy and soak into the surrounding food.

Potato Some varieties of potato go leathery in pre-cooked frozen dishes unless they are mashed first.

Salad ingredients Lettuce, endive, watercress, spring onions, celery, cress, chicory, radish, cucumber and tomato go limp and mushy if frozen—and there is no way of getting their crispness back.

Sauces It is wise to keep the thickening of sauces to a minimum and use beurre manié or thickening granules when reheating.

Single cream (that is, with less than 35 per cent butter fat) separates on thawing. It may go back to normal with excessive whipping but this is unlikely, so it is better not to freeze in the first place. See page 30 for directions for freezing double cream.

Yogurt that is homemade or natural separates when frozen. Flavoured sweet yogurts show little or no deterioration.

FREEZER FACTS

TYPES OF FREEZER

The type of freezer you choose will depend on the amount of space you have to put it in and what kind of food you plan to store, so it is important to buy the type that suits you best.

Upright Freezers
The same shape as a full-size refrigerator, these range in size from small, table top models to large upright ones. They have front opening doors—large freezers sometimes have two doors with compartments that operate independently to each other—take up less floor space than chest freezers and are less obtrusive. An upright freezer may be twinned with a matching refrigerator.

Chest Freezers
Size for size, chest freezers are cheaper than upright models, and running costs are lower, since the cold air does not escape on door opening to the same extent as an upright freezer. They have an additional advantage too: more food will fit into the same amount of space, since large items can be accommodated with small ones tucked in around them, unrestricted by shelves and baskets. They do take up considerably more floor space; are more difficult to keep organised (although baskets do help) and small people or those with bad backs will find it difficult to reach down to the bottom of the cabinet.

Economy models are available. These have thicker wall insulation, therefore saving energy, and give better performance in the event of a power cut—the only drawback is an increased level of CFCs.

Fridge/Freezers
A unit which incorporates a refrigerator and a freezer. There are three to four different types, those with top mount freezers, bottom mount freezers, and horizontal fridge/freezers. Some have equal capacity splits, others have a larger freezer than refrigerator and vice versa. Some have two compressors, making it possible for the refrigerator or freezer to be used independently—the refrigerator may be switched off when going on holiday.

Frost-Free Freezers
This is a relatively new feature in the UK, but common in America and Japan. It incorporates a fan to force air around the cabinet, thereby stopping the moisture in the air from settling on the food and walls of the freezer. It is available in upright freezers and fridge/freezers.

The advantages of owning a frost-free cabinet are no defrosting, faster freezing, foods that don't stick together, labels remain clear and easy to read, ice doesn't build up and restrict capacity, and freezer temperatures are more accurately maintained. However, size for size, capacities tend to be smaller than the equivalent static model.

POINTS TO LOOK FOR

Before buying, check the models you are interested in carefully. See how easy it will be to open the door when the freezer is in position in your home—it is sometimes possible to buy the same model with the door hung on the other side.

Can you reach the top shelf of an upright model and the bottom corners of a chest easily? Look at the position of the controls: are they simple to use? Could they be altered by an inquisitive child?

Has the freezer got a lock—probably necessary if you are going to keep it in a garage or shed—and do you need an interior light?

A drainage hole is useful in a chest freezer–check it has one so that you don't have to bale out when defrosting.

A good upright freezer should incorporate a defrost spout for defrosting, with baffles or solid fronts on drawers/compartments to stop cold air escaping as soon as the door is opened. Drawers that don't tip and fall when full are important, and removable drawers for added flexibility.

Check the type of door handle, for example, a flush handle when children are about, or a handle that protrudes maybe better for the elderly. If the freezer is not under a worktop, is there a grille at the back to stop small objects falling down behind?

Look too for rollers, which enable you to slide the freezer out to clean behind and beneath it, or for adjustable levelling feet if your floor is uneven. Check what is the maximum amount of fresh food that can be frozen in 24 hours.

Finally check the energy consumption figures. Types and models vary.

The Star Symbols
All freezers must carry this star symbol ✳ ✳✳✳ which indicates that they are capable of freezing down fresh food. An appliance with three stars or less is suitable only for storing ready frozen food:

The Fast-Freeze Switch

> ✳ for 1 week at $-6°C$
> ✳✳ for 1 month at $-12°C$
> ✳✳✳ for 3 months at $-18°C$

The fast-freeze switch works by overriding the thermostat. It allows the temperature to fall to $-28°C$ while the rest of the frozen food does not exceed $-18°C$.

The food freezes faster in the colder temperature and because smaller ice crystals are formed the texture of the food will be better when thawed. Reducing the temperature means, too, that the food already in the freezer gets colder and will be less affected by the higher temperature of the fresh food. Turn on the fast-freeze switch about 6 hours before you plan to put in food to be frozen, then leave it on for up to 12 to 24 hours to freeze the food (see page 17).

Some models also incorporate a light to indicate when fast-freeze is on, this is a useful feature reducing the risk of fast-freeze being left on for days at a time.

Some frost-free models do not incorporate a fast-freeze switch but the manufacturers will suggest a position within the cabinet for fast freezing which is colder due to the position of the cold air fan.

It is possible to freeze down food, especially in small quantities, without using the fast-freeze switch, but the faster the food is frozen the better it will taste.

Freezer Size
The freezer capacity is quoted in either cubic litres or feet. (To make a rough comparison divide the number of litres by 30 to give the number of cubic feet (1 cubic foot = 28.3 litres).) Some manufacturers quote capacity in gross volume and some in net, so watch out for this.

How large a freezer you need depends on a number of factors: for instance, how often you shop; whether you plan to cook for your freezer or merely to store basic ingredients; how many people there are in the household, and whether you will be freezing your own produce.

It is generally suggested that you should allow 56 litres (2 cubic feet) per person plus 56 extra litres (2 cubic feet) but do think carefully about your particular needs before deciding. Talk to friends who own freezers to see whether they are satisfied with the size they have. If in doubt buy a model that is 28–56 litres (1 or 2 cubic feet) larger than you think you need—you will probably use the extra capacity.

SITING AND INSTALLING A FREEZER

Siting a Freezer

The most convenient place for a freezer is obviously in or near the kitchen, but it can be sited anywhere in the home, or even in a garage or shed. Bear in mind, though, that it does make a certain amount of noise which may rule out a dining room or bedroom. Also do not position near a heat source. Chest freezers take up a lot of space but are unlikely to provide the same amount of worktop area as you will need to be able to open it. Upright freezers may need more than their width in order to be able to open the door properly: on some models the door must be opened more than 90 degrees before you can pull out the baskets. Also you need to allow about 5 cm (2 inches) at the back for ventilation.

If siting a freezer upstairs, be careful that it is not tilted to an angle of more than 30 degrees from upright while it is being moved or you may get an airlock in the coolant. A chest freezer should always be positioned across the joists if upstairs otherwise it may damage the floorboards.

If the freezer is to be sited in a garage or shed, it is best to put it on strong bricks or solid pieces of wood to prevent it getting damp and rusting. Any freezer which is kept in an out-of-the-way place should be fitted with a freezer alarm so that you get a warning if anything goes wrong, such as a blown fuse. Check before siting the freezer in a garage, outhouse or very cold north facing kitchen as some are not designed to operate in temperatures below 16°C (61°F).

Installing a Freezer

All you need to run a freezer is a 13-amp socket outlet. But there are a number of things you must do before you plug in your freezer for the first time.

First of all make sure there is a socket outlet close–you don't want metres of extension lead running through your home. It is worth paying to have a suitable socket fitted and at the same time putting the freezer on a separate circuit from the rest of the house. This means that you can switch off all electricity except the freezer supply when you go away for a few days.

If you are plugging a freezer into one half of a double socket outlet do not use the other half for appliances, such as food processors or coffee grinders, which are plugged in and unplugged frequently, because you may accidentally unplug the freezer. It is a good idea to cover the socket switch and the freezer's plug with tape to deter unplugging. Alternatively, fit a plug which incorporates an automatic buzzer if the socket is switched off.

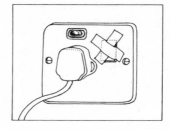

Cover the switch of your freezer with adhesive tape to prevent it being accidentally switched off.

Make sure your freezer is in position with the correct air gap behind and around it (check the handbook) and that the feet are either levelled up if they are adjustable or packed up with small pieces of hardboard. Use a spirit level.

Wipe the interior of the freezer with a solution of 15 ml (1 tbsp) bicarbonate of soda to 1 litre (1¾ pints) warm water and dry it thoroughly. After the freezer has been moved into position, allow the oil in the compressor to settle for several hours before switching on (leave the door open).

Once your have turned it on and it is running normally, put in some food, then check that the freezer is maintaining the right temperature. Use a freezer thermometer and move it to a different position every 24 hours to see if there are any spots which are particularly cold or warm. Set the thermostat so that all parts of the freezer maintain a temperature of −18°C (0°F) or less. There is no need to keep the freezer colder than this except when you are using the fast-freeze switch (see page 17).

DEFROSTING A FREEZER

Defrost your freezer when the frost on the walls reaches a thickness of 0.5 cm (¼ inch). Follow the manufacturer's instructions for the procedure. You will need a plastic spatula to tap the frost loose as it melts, some old towels to mop up with and bowls of hot water to speed up the process.

Try to defrost when your stocks are low or when it is a cold day. Put the contents of the freezer in the refrigerator, a cool box or wrap it in newspapers or old blankets.

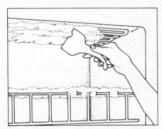

Use a plastic spatula to defrost. Never use a metal implement as this will damage the freezer surface.

Avoid a flood by using a sheet of foil to funnel melting ice into a bowl.

When the freezer is defrosted, wash out with a solution of 15 ml (1 tbsp) bicarbonate of soda to 1 litre (1¾ pints) water.

When the freezer is free of frost, wash it out with a solution of 15 ml (1 tbsp) bicarbonate of soda to 1 litre (1¾ pints) warm water. Dry the cabinet thoroughly before switching on again.

Maintain the outside of the freezer by wiping it over occasionally with a solution of washing-up liquid and warm water. Always dry it thoroughly. Use the crevice tool on the vacuum cleaner to remove dust from the network of pipes at the back, taking care not to damage them. Clean the door seals regularly, rotten door seals will eventually lead to higher running costs as the cold air escapes from them. If the freezer is in a garage or shed, polish it from time to time with a silicon all-purpose polish to help it resist damp.

FREEZER MAINTENANCE

Running Costs

Running costs are hard to estimate as they will vary according to the warmth of the room the freezer is sited in. It is possible to get a rough idea of the running costs by checking the wattage on the rating plate at the back of the freezer. Look at the figure before the 'w' or 'W'. If it is in watts divide it by 1000 to give the kW rating, then multiply this figure by the current cost of a unit of electricity—this will give you the running cost for an hour. However, the freezer is only using electricity when the compressor is pumping the coolant round the system, so the actual running costs will be much lower than this.

You can keep the costs down by following a few simple measures:

- Do not site the freezer near a central heating boiler, hob or oven, or where direct sunlight will fall on it.

- Open the freezer door/lid as little as possible.

- Only put cold food into the freezer.

It may be worth buying a freezer alarm, which sounds if the door has not been shut properly.

Breakdowns

Freezers are generally reliable but they may break down from time to time. Before you call a service engineer, check the following points:

* Is there a power cut?
  Check by switching on a light.

* Is the socket outlet working?
  Plug in another appliance and check.

* Has the fuse in the plug blown?
  Change it and see.

* Is the compressor working?
  Switch to fast-freeze and listen, if there is no noise it is not working.

If the freezer seems very cold you may have left the fast-freeze switch on, or accidentally knocked the thermostat setting. If it sounds very noisy, check that the freezer has not been pushed too close to the wall and that it is level.

You may be able to repair a faulty door seal or perished rubber pads by the compressor—you should be able to buy the spare parts from the manufacturer.

Power Cuts

Provided you take certain precautions, food in a chest freezer will remain undamaged for about 48 hours without power if you have had advanced warning and 30–35 hours without. An upright freezer will keep the contents safe for about 26 hours with advance warning, 30 hours without.

If there is advance warning of a power cut at least 6 hours before it occurs, turn on the fast-freeze switch, but first make sure the freezer is full—fill any gaps with rolled-up newspaper, old towels or plastic boxes filled with water.

Do not open the door during a power cut as this will let warm air into the freezer.

Cover the freezer with a blanket to increase its insulation but make sure the condenser and pipes at the back are left clear.

Once the power has been restored, leave the freezer on fast-freeze (or switch to it if there has been no advanced warning) for at least 2 hours.

Some manufacturers provide cold accumulators in some models. These help increase the hold over time in the event of a power cut. Alternatively, store three or four freezer cold blocks in your freezer.

The contents of your freezer can be worth a considerable amount of money and it is worth looking into freezer insurance. Several insurance companies offer freezer insurance as part of a household contents policy while others issue a separate policy. In either case, check exactly what is covered.

Reducing Losses

It is not always necessary to throw out all the food from your freezer if there has been a lengthy power cut or breakdown. Some thawed uncooked foods can be cooked, then refrozen.

Once food has begun to thaw bacteria multiply more rapidly than in the equivalent fresh food. It is important to cook the food as soon as possible. Some freezers incorporate thermal indicators which tell you whether the temperature has gone above 0°C (32°F). If you are sure that the temperature of the freezer has not gone over 0°C (32°F) the food can be refrozen by switching on the fast-freeze switch for a few hours. The items which are most likely to be affected by thawing are meat, poultry and fish, so if these seem to have thawed out too much, cook and then freeze them. Be sure to thaw any you do not cook in a refrigerator, then cook as soon as they are thawed.

Re-Freezing Partly Thawed Food

Do not re-freeze food once it has thawed, unless you have subsequently cooked it. For example, it is perfectly safe to thaw red meat or fish, use it to make a casserole and then re-freeze it. Never re-freeze food that has thawed accidentally over a period of days, or food that has already been thawed and reheated.

If you return home from holiday and find the freezer off and food lying in a puddle, the safest thing is to discard the whole lot.

Guarantees and Maintenance Contracts

When you buy your freezer it will have a guarantee, usually a year. Some manufacturers allow you to extend the guarantee to 5 years on payment of an extra sum at the time of purchase. Before you pay this, check that the extended guarantee covers both parts and labour. Sometimes only the compressor is covered, with the other parts of the freezer guaranteed for only one year.

When the guarantee period expires you will have to decide whether or not to take up the manufacturer's offer of a maintenance contract. Look carefully at the terms of the contract to see what is covered—both parts and labour should be if it is to be worthwhile. Make sure too that a daily emergency service operates. You may decide it is better to save the annual cost of the maintenance contract and put the money towards a repair or new freezer.

Moving House

If possible it is best to empty the freezer if it is to be moved, as a full freezer is very heavy. Some removal firms do have the facility to plug a loaded freezer into an electrical supply in their van; if you want to do this, the freezer should be the last item into the van and the first one out.

When moving a freezer it should be kept as upright as possible and never tipped at an angle of more than 30 degrees as this could cause an airlock in the cooling system. When it is unloaded and installed, switch the freezer on to check that all the lights work, then turn it off and let the oil in the compressor settle down for 2 or 3 hours before running it. When you sign the removal firm's documents stating that the job has been completed, write a note to the effect that the freezer has not been tested.

BUYING A SECONDHAND FREEZER

A secondhand freezer can be a good buy but you should check it carefully first. Make sure it can freeze down food and not simply store frozen food, check how old it is—if over 5 years it may just be reaching the point where things start to go wrong. Look for signs of rust; check all the controls work and test the door seal by shutting a piece of paper in the door and seeing whether it moves easily or not. Some shops sell reconditioned freezers.

Disposing of an Old Freezer or Fridge/Freezer

There are a number of dangers to families and the environment involved in the disposal of your old cabinet.

Firstly, it is imperative to ensure that a child cannot get into the old cabinet, this is particularly true of chest freezers and those with locks. Ensure that the old cabinet is well sealed and out of harms way.

Secondly, some manufacturers, electrical retailers and local authorities will extract the CFCs from the system and return it to the chemical manufacturer for recycling. This, of course, reduces the quantity of CFCs being released into the environment.

About 80% of the CFCs in the cabinet are in the insulation material. Whilst this material can be treated at very high temperatures to produce less harmful gases, this is not currently done in the UK.

FREEZER PACKAGING

Good packaging is vital if food in the freezer is to remain in good condition. Freezing converts the water content of the food to ice crystals which must be retained, as they are converted back to moisture when the food is thawed. Badly packed food will dry out causing white patches known as 'freezer burn'. There is also a risk that strong-smelling foods will transfer their odours to other foods. Although it is important to store all frozen food correctly, any which is to be stored for a long time must be extremely well wrapped, since it will tend to get pushed around when other items are put into and removed from the freezer.

When choosing packaging materials, it is worth considering whether or not you will want to thaw or reheat the food in a microwave. Anything wrapped or packed in foil will need to be transferred to another container before it can be put in a microwave. (See Thawing Frozen Food in the Microwave on page 43.)

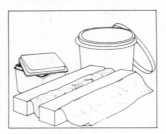

Careful packaging is essential if food is to remain in good condition.

PACKING MATERIALS

Foil

This is very useful for wrapping because it can be shaped to cover awkward items and moulded closely around the food to ensure air does not get in. Use a single layer of the standard thickness or a double layer if you are using thin kitchen foil. Seal it by folding the edges closely over each other, if necessary using freezer tape.

Foil should not be used for wrapping acidic fruits which may react with it. If you think the foil is likely to become punctured in the freezer, overwrap large items with a polythene bag.

Fatty foods like cheese and uncooked blocks of pastry are best wrapped in greaseproof paper and overwrapped in foil.

Polythene Bags and Sheeting

Both polythene bags and sheeting can be used for freezer wrapping; the bags, available in a variety of sizes, are easier to use than sheeting which needs careful wrapping and sealing. Use heavy-gauge polythene which will protect the food, rather than the thin bags used for packing sandwiches and keeping food in the refrigerator. Most foods can be stored in polythene bags, but liquids and solids-plus-liquids such as stews, should be frozen in a polythene bag placed in a container (see page 18). The square or rectangular shapes produced are compact to store in the freezer.

Squeeze out as much air as possible from the bags before they are put in the freezer; or suck it out with a straw or vacuum pump. Seal the bags with freezer tape or twist ties.

Freezer Wrap

Plastic wrap tends to cling to itself and also to plastic and metal so is very useful when wrapping food for the freezer. Use it as a lining if you want to pack acidic fruits in foil and also for wrapping individual portions of foods which can then be stored together in a polythene bag and removed one at a time. Always overwrap in polythene bags in case the wrap becomes loose. Do not use plastic wrap if thawing the food in the microwave as the plasticiser in ordinary cling film can migrate into the food if it is used in the microwave.

Foil Dishes

Foil dishes come in a range of sizes and shapes and you can cook, freeze and reheat food in them. Used and cleaned carefully they can be recycled several times, but the lids should only be used once. Foil dishes cannot be used in the microwave.

Foil containers come in a range of shapes and sizes.

Plastic Containers

These are more expensive than other types of freezer packaging, but will last for years. Some varieties may lose their airtight seal after a while and need sealing with freezer tape to prevent air affecting the contents. While you may want special plastic shapes for some foods, ice cream bombes for instance, square and rectangular containers make better use of freezer space than round ones.

Other Packaging

Packaging containers from some bought foods are useful in the freezer though not in the microwave. Good examples are margarine tubs, yogurt and cream pots and foil dishes. Make sure they are scrupulously clean and do not expect them to survive more than two or three times. Use freezer tape to ensure an airtight seal.

Most glass is unsuitable for use in the freezer because it is likely to shatter. Specially toughened glass dishes are handy for mousses and desserts which are to be served in the dish, but they *must* be freezerproof.

In addition to wraps, bags and boxes you will also needs sheets of waxed or non-stick paper; plastic- or paper-covered wire twists ties which can be bought ready-cut or on a roll; freezer tape; labels; a chinagraph or waterproof felt pen.

Dishes for Freezer and Microwave

When necessary, pack food in containers that are suitable for both the freezer and the microwave. Freezer-to-oven microwave, designed especially for freezing conventionally cooked foods to be reheated in the microwave, is now increasingly available. Cardboard-type cartons are ideal for pies, flans and non-liquid dishes which need microwaving only for a short time, but it can only be used once. Boil in the bags and roasting bags, which are ideal for freezing casseroles, vegetables and small joints, can both be put directly into the microwave.

PACKING IN MANAGEABLE QUANTITIES

It is very important to pack food so that you can easily remove the amount you want from the freezer. Chops and pancakes, for example, should be frozen with paper interleaved between them, then wrapped, so that you can remove only the number you require. Casseroles and pâtés are best frozen in relatively small quantities—you can then thaw as many packs as you need.

Soups, stock and sauces should not be frozen in quantities larger than 600 ml (1 pint). Freezing liquid in ice-cube trays and storing the cubes in polythene bags is a good way of retrieving a minute quantity when required. With free-flow items, such as peas or beans, you can just pour out the amount needed.

SEALING

Once you have first extracted all the air from polythene bags of food for freezing, twist ties or freezer tape are an excellent way of sealing. Twist ties with metal closures should be removed before putting food in the microwave. Freezer tape has a

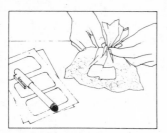

Pack and label food carefully before freezing.

special adhesive that sticks at low temperatures, unlike ordinary sticky tape, and is available in white, which you can write on and save the extra cost of labels.

Heat sealing is a very secure method of sealing polythene bags and is particularly useful if you want to use the packet as a 'boil-in-the-bag' item. You can buy special electric sealers for freezer bags, although it is probably not worth investing in one unless you use it regularly.

LABELLING

It is essential to label everything that goes into your freezer, unless it is a commercial packet which clearly states what the contents are. However convinced you are that you will be able to tell bortsch from blackcurrant sorbet when you put them in, after a few months they will seem identical. You will need to use a chinagraph pencil or waterproof felt-tipped pen for labelling, so that the information does not become rubbed or wiped off. Some polythene bags have a white label printed on them; on other items you will need to use a special freezer label with an adhesive which sticks at low temperatures. On each packet write the contents, quantity and date of freezing.

Ideally you should add the expiry date according to the maximum recommended storage time. Aim to rotate food in the freezer every 3 months as a general rule.

If other people are going to cook and eat the food, it may be worth including brief instructions about thawing, reheating and any extra ingredients which should be added. You can buy freezer labels in different colours so that you can code things for easier finding—for example red for meat, green for vegetables, and so on.

How to Freeze

Freezing is a very simple process, based on how quickly heat can be taken out of food (*not* cold pumped in), but unless you grasp the basics, it is possible to make some equally simple mistakes. These rarely make the food inedible, but they may affect its taste, texture, colour and—most vital of all if you are feeding a young growing family—its food value.

Most foods are largely made up of water, even something as seemingly solid as lean meat contains about 70 per cent water. All freezing does is convert this water to ice crystals. Quick freezing results in tiny ice crystals, retained within the cell structure, so that on thawing, the structure is undamaged and the food value unchanged. But slow freezing results in the formation of large ice crystals, which damage the cell structure and cause loss of nutrients. This damage is irreversible, and slow-frozen food shows loss of texture, colour and flavour when thawed. Foods like cucumber and strawberries, which have a high water content, never freeze successfully because even the tiniest crystal formation breaks down their delicate structure.

To avoid slow freezing, never freeze more than one-tenth of your freezer's capacity in any 24 hours or else not only will heat be absorbed by the freezer's refrigeration system, but also by food already frozen. If, for instance, you have a 50 kg (110 lb) freezer (approximately 170 litres or 6 cubic feet), you should only ever freeze about 5 kg (11 lb) of food at a time. If you freeze more, the addition of the unfrozen food pushes up the freezer temperature and the result will be *slow-frozen food*.

Using the Fast-Freeze Switch

Not all manufacturers give clear instructions on how to use the fast-freeze switch (see page 9) so here is a guide:

For small amounts, such as one loaf plus one small casserole, it is probably not necessary to use the switch, simply add the food. This should be safe for up to about 4 items but not including anything as dense as a leg of lamb.

For a fairly small amount, such as 4 casseroles and 3 pies, put on the fast-freeze switch for about 2 hours before putting the food in. Leave it on for about 4 hours afterwards.

For a large amount, such as half a carcass of fresh meat, put on the fast-freeze switch for about 6 hours beforehand to ensure the freezer is really cold. Put the packaged meat in and leave the switch on for a further 12–24 hours, depending on the load.

Some freezers have a separate freezing-in compartment. This is generally the coldest part of the cabinet and is separate from the main cabinet. The division will also prevent warmish food coming into contact with what is already frozen and starting a slight thaw.

If your freezer has no separate compartment, put the food against the sides or base, or on a shelf that carries the evaporator coils—that is, in the coldest possible part of the freezer.

FREEZING SOLIDS

Package solids tightly, so that you expel as much air as possible, wrapping them in foil or freezer wrap, which fits where it touches. If filling a rigid container and the food only comes halfway up, fill up the vacant space with crumpled foil or non-stick paper. Half-empty containers waste freezer space, though, so try to avoid this.

It is even more difficult to expel air from a polythene bag, especially when the contents are awkwardly shaped or easily

Keep a supply of moisture and vapour-proof containers suitable for the freezer.

broken. Squeeze out as much air as possible (see also page 14).

FREEZING LIQUIDS

Liquid expands one tenth when frozen, so it is essential to leave at least 1 cm (½ inch) of 'headspace' in a container holding about 300 ml (½ pint) and about 2.5 cm (1 inch) for a container holding 600 ml (1 pint). Unless you leave room for expansion, items such as soups, sauces and fruits packed in syrup will push off their lids.

If you use a strong, freezerproof glass container, make sure it has straight sides, as it is easier to get the frozen contents out again, and leave 2.5–5 cm (1–2 inches) headspace.

FREEZING SOLIDS AND LIQUIDS

Combinations of solids and liquids, stews and casseroles or fruit in syrup, should if possible have a layer of liquid on the top, with no pieces of food sticking out. Leave 1 cm (½ inch) of headspace. Solids which rise above the surface of the liquid, such as fruit salad, need an inner covering of crumpled non-stick paper before wrapping.

PREFORMING

This is ideal for storing liquid foods such as fruit purées, casseroles and stocks in a polythene bag, rather than a rigid container. The food is placed in a polythene bag-lined container, frozen until solid, then removed from the container. The food is

then in a neat, regular shape for storing in the freezer, and the container can be used for other things.

Foil is also ideal for this method if you want to end up with a neatly shaped casserole. Of course, you can freeze food in its casserole dish but if you want to keep the dish in circulation, preforming is the answer. Cook the casserole first. Line another casserole with foil, leaving a good margin for wrapping over; spoon in the contents. Once solid, slip out the package and fold the foil over, then overwrap with a

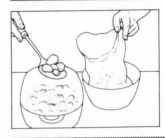

Freeze casseroles in a polythene bag inside a rigid container. Remove the container when the food is solid.

polythene bag before freezing. Place the unwrapped package back into the original casserole for reheating (if the foil tends to stick, dip the package in warm water for just a minute or two). (An alternative method is to cook the food in the casserole, freeze it, then dip the casserole in warm water just long enough to loosen the contents, which can then be removed and wrapped in the usual way.)
Note: Unless the casserole is straight sided and lipless, the contents may not be removed very easily.

FREEZING VEGETABLES

Vegetables for freezing should just have reached maturity; the carbohydrate content of peas and beans, for instance, changes from starch to sugar at this point.

Vegetables need to be blanched before freezing to destroy the enzyme present, to preserve the colour, flavour and texture and, to a certain extent, to reduce the micro-organisms present; it also helps to retain their vitamin C content.

The vegetables should be prepared as if for cooking, then blanched in not less than 4 litres (7 pints) boiling water to each 450 g (1 lb), with 10 ml (2 tsp) salt. The water must return to the boil in 1 minute after the vegetables are added. The blanching water can be used six or seven times, thus achieving less loss of minerals and a vitamin C build-up in the blanching water. After this time, replace with fresh water. Do not blanch more than 450 g (1 lb) at a time.

A blanching basket makes blanching easier.

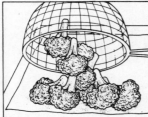

Drain cooled, blanched vegetables on a clean tea towel.

Follow the times in the chart on pages 20–22. Calculate from the time the water reboils. A blanching basket makes the process easier.

After blanching, remove the vegetables at once and plunge them into ice-cold water (add ice cubes to the water) to prevent overcooking and to cool as quickly as possible. Cooling time is usually the same as the blanching time. For each batch, use fresh iced water. Drain in a colander immediately the vegetables are cool. Careful timing ensures the best results, so a kitchen timer or watch with a second hand is essential. (See also Blanching in the Microwave on page 48.)

Note: In an emergency—for example, when dealing with a glut crop—vegetables can be frozen unblanched but this method is not to be generally recommended.

The following can be frozen without blanching and kept for the times stated:

Brussels sprouts	3 days
Broad beans	3 weeks
Runner beans	5 months
Sweetcorn	1 month
Peppers	3 months
Peas	6–9 months
Carrots	12 months
Spinach	12 months

PREPARING VEGETABLES FOR FREEZING

Vegetable	Preparation	Blanching
Artichokes, globe	Remove all outer coarse leaves and stalks, and trim tops and stems. Wash well in cold water, add a little lemon juice to the blanching water. Cool, drain upside-down on absorbent kitchen paper. Pack in rigid containers.	Blanch, a few at a time, in a large container for 8–10 minutes. Fonds only 4–5 minutes.
Asparagus	Grade into thick and thin stems but do not tie into bunches yet. Wash in cold water, blanch, cool and drain. Tie into small bundles. Pack in rigid containers.	Thin stems—2 minutes Thick stems—4 minutes
Aubergines	Peel and cut roughly into 2.5 cm (1 inch) slices. Blanch, chill and dry on absorbent kitchen paper. Pack in layers, separated by non-stick paper.	3–4 minutes
Avocados	Prepare in pulp form: peel and mash, allowing 15 ml (1 tbsp) lemon juice to each avocado. Pack in small containers. Also good frozen with full fat soft cheese to use as a party dip.	
Beans French, runner, broad	Select young, tender beans; wash thoroughly. French—trim ends and blanch. Runner—slice thickly and blanch. Broad—shell and blanch. In each case, cool, drain and pack.	2–3 minutes 2 minutes 3 minutes
Beetroot	Choose small beets up to 5 cm (2 inch) diameter. Wash well and rub skin off after blanching. Beetroot under 2.5 cm (1 inch) in diameter may be frozen whole; others should be sliced or diced. Pack in rigid containers. *Note:* Short blanching and long storage can make beetroot rubbery.	Small whole—5–10 minutes Large—cook until tender—45–50 minutes
Broccoli	Trim off any woody parts and large leaves. Wash in salted water, cut into small florets. Blanch, cool and drain well. Pack in rigid containers in 1–2 layers, tips to stalks.	Thin stems—3 minutes Medium stems—4 minutes Thick stems—5 minutes
Brussels sprouts	Use small compact heads. Remove outer leaves and wash thoroughly. Make small cuts in stem. Blanch, cool and drain well before packing.	Small—3 minutes Medium—4 minutes
Cabbage green, red	Use only young, crisp, well-hearted cabbage. Wash thoroughly, shred. Blanch, cool and drain. Pack in small quantities in polythene bags.	1–2 minutes
Carrots	Choose small young carrots. If left whole, scrape after blanching. Slice or cut into small dice. Blanch, cool, drain and pack.	3–5 minutes

Preparing Vegetables for Freezing continued

Vegetable	Preparation	Blanching
Cauliflower	Heads should be firm, compact and white. Wash, break into small florets, about 5 cm (2 inches) in diameter. Add the juice of a lemon to the blanching water to keep them white; blanch, cool, drain and pack.	3 minutes
Celeriac	Wash and trim. Cook until almost tender, peel and slice. Cool, then pack.	
Celery	Trim, removing any strings, and scrub well. Cut into 2.5 cm (1 inch) lengths. Suitable only for cooked dishes.	2 minutes
Chestnuts	Wash nuts, cover with water, bring to the boil, drain and peel. Pack in rigid containers. Can be used to supplement raw chestnuts in recipe, or cooked and frozen as purée in soups and sweets.	1–2 minutes
Chillies	Remove stalks and scoop out the seeds and pithy part. Blanch, cool, drain and pack.	2 minutes
Corn on the cob	Select young yellow kernels, not starchy, over-ripe or shrunken. Remove husks and 'silks'. Blanch, cool and dry. Pack individually in greaseproof paper or foil.	Small—4 minutes Medium—6 minutes Large—8 minutes
Courgettes	Choose young ones. Wash and cut into 1 cm (1/2 inch) slices. Either blanch or sauté in a little butter.	1 minute
Fennel	Trim and cut into short lengths. Blanch, cool, drain and pack.	2 minutes
Kohlrabi	Use small roots, 5–7.5 cm (2–3 inches) in diameter. Cut off tops, peel and dice. Blanch, cool, drain and pack.	1 1/2 minutes
Leeks	Cut off tops and roots; remove coarse outside leaves. Slice into 1 cm (1/2 inch) slices and wash well. Sauté in butter or oil for 4 minutes. Drain, cool, pack and freeze. Only suitable for casseroles or as a base to vichysoisse.	
Mange-tout	Trim the ends. Blanch, cool, drain and pack. Use only young tender produce.	2 minutes
Marrow	Young marrows can be peeled, cut into 1–2.5 cm (1/2–1 inch) slices and blanched before packing.	3 minutes
Mushrooms	Choose small button mushrooms and leave whole. Wipe clean but don't peel or blanch. Sauté in butter for 1 minute. Mushrooms larger than 2.5 cm (1 inch) in diameter are suitable only for slicing and using in cooked dishes.	

Preparing Vegetables for Freezing continued

Vegetable	Preparation	Blanching
Onions	Can be peeled, finely chopped and packed in small polythene containers for cooking later; packages should be overwrapped, to prevent the smell filtering out. *Note:* Small onions may be blanched whole and used later in casseroles.	2 minutes Small whole—4 minutes
Parsnips	Trim and peel young parsnips, then cut into narrow strips. Blanch, cool and dry.	2 minutes
Peas, green	Use young, sweet green peas, not old or starchy. Shell and blanch. Shake the blanching basket from time to time to distribute the heat evenly. Cool, drain and pack in polythene bags or rigid containers.	1–2 minutes
Peppers	Freeze red and green peppers separately. Wash well, remove stems and all traces of seeds and membranes. Can be blanched as halves for stuffed peppers, or in thin slices for stews and casseroles. For better colour, when storage is less than 6 months, do not blanch.	3 minutes
Potatoes	Best frozen in the cooked form, as partially-cooked chips (fully-cooked ones are not satisfactory), croquettes or duchesse potatoes. New: choose small even-sized potatoes. Scrape, cook fully with mint and cool. (Appearance similar to that of canned potatoes.) Chipped: Soak in cold water for about 30 minutes. Drain, dry. Part deep-fry for 2 minutes, cool and freeze for final frying.	
Spinach	Select young leaves. Wash very thoroughly under running water; drain. Blanch in small quantities, cool quickly and press out excess moisture, or purée. Pack in rigid containers or polythene bags.	2 minutes
Tomatoes	Tomatoes are most useful if frozen as purée. Small whole tomatoes, packed in bags, can be used in cooked dishes. To make tomato purée, skin and core tomatoes. Simmer in their own juice for 5 minutes until soft. Rub through a nylon sieve or purée in a blender. Cool and pack in small containers.	
Turnips	Use small, young turnips. Trim, peel, then cut into small dice, about 1 cm ($^1/_2$ inch). Blanch, cool, drain and pack in rigid containers. *Note:* Turnips may be fully cooked and mashed before freezing—leave 1 cm ($^1/_2$ inch) headspace.	$2^1/_2$ minutes

Unsuitable for freezing: Chicory, cucumber, endive, kale, lettuce, radishes, Jerusalem artichokes (suitable only as soups and purées).

FREEZING FRUIT

Fruits should be frozen just as they
become ready for eating, though slightly
over-ripe fruits can be frozen as purées. It
is best to choose unblemished, fresh fruit.
Lightly wash and dry well, if necessary. Do
not freeze in contact with any metal,
including foil. If blanching, blanch as
vegetables, without the salt. There are four
basic methods for freezing fruit: dry (free
flow) pack, dry sugar pack, syrup pack and
purée.

Dry Pack

Fruits like blackcurrants, gooseberries,
blackberries and raspberries, which do not
discolour easily, can be frozen just as they
are. Spread the fruit on baking trays or
sheets lined with non-stick or greaseproof
paper and put into the freezer until
frozen—this is known as open freezing.
Pack the frozen fruit in polythene bags.
The fruit will stay separate or 'free-flow', so
that small amounts can be used as required.

Dry Sugar Pack

Fruits like the above can be sprinkled with
sugar before freezing, then as they thaw
the liquid and sugar make a syrup. Spread
the fruit in a shallow dish and sprinkle with
caster sugar, allowing 50 g (2 oz) sugar to
each 450 g (1 lb) fruit. Gently mix. Pack in
rigid containers, leaving 1–2 cm ($^{1}/_{2}$–$^{3}/_{4}$
inch) headspace.

Syrup Pack

Firm-textured fruits like peaches and
apricots which are likely to discolour
easily, particularly on thawing, are best
frozen in a sugar syrup.

As a rough guide, allow 300 ml ($^{1}/_{2}$ pint)
syrup for every 450 g (1 lb) fruit. Dissolve
the sugar in the water, bring to the boil and
remove from the heat. Add lemon juice
where indicated, then cover and leave to
cool. Pour the syrup over the fruit or place
the fruit in a container with the syrup. Light
fruits which tend to rise in liquids can be
held below the surface by using a
dampened and crumpled piece of non-
absorbent paper, such as greaseproof, on
top of the mixture. Leave 1–2 cm ($^{1}/_{2}$–$^{3}/_{4}$
inch) headspace for expansion.

Fruits that discolour, such as apples and
pears, should first be soaked in a solution
of lemon juice. Use the juice of 1 lemon to
each 1 litre ($1^{3}/_{4}$ pints) water used. When
preparing large quantities of fruit, make the
syrup the day before and leave to chill
overnight, as it has to be used cold.

Purée

Over-ripe fruit can be puréed in a blender
or food processor, then sieved to remove
seeds if necessary. Pack in rigid
containers, leaving 1–2 cm ($^{1}/_{2}$–$^{3}/_{4}$ inch)
headspace for expansion. Cover purées
with a layer of freezer wrap if they are
likely to discolour. Purées make good
standby sauces and desserts.

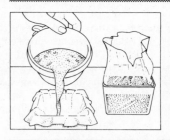

*Freeze fruit
purées in a
polythene bag
placed inside
a rigid
container.
Remove the
container when
the food is
solid.*

23

PREPARING FRUIT FOR FREEZING

Fruit	*Preparation*
Apples, sliced	Peel, core and drop into cold water. Cut into 0.5 cm ($^1/_4$ inch) slices. Blanch for 2–3 minutes and cool in ice-cold water before packing. Useful for pies and flans.
purée	Peel, core and stew in the minimum amount of water, sweetened or unsweetened. Purée or mash. Leave to cool before packing.
Apricots	Plunge into boiling water for 30 seconds to loosen the skins, then peel. Use one of the following methods: (a) Cut in half or slice into syrup made with 450 g (1 lb) sugar to 1 litre (2 pints) water, with some lemon juice added to prevent browning; for each 450 g (1 lb) pack allow the juice of 1 lemon. Immerse the apricots by placing a piece of clean, crumpled non-absorbent paper on the fruit, under the lid. (b) Leave whole and freeze in cold syrup. After long storage, an almond flavour may develop round the stone. (c) Purée cooked apricots, sweetened and unsweetened. Pack in rigid containers.
Berries (including currants and cherries)	All may be frozen by the dry pack method, but the dry sugar pack method is suitable for soft fruits, such as raspberries. *Dry Pack:* Sort the fruit; some whole berries may be left on their sprigs or stems for use as decoration. Spread the fruit on paper-lined trays or baking sheets, open freeze, then pack. *Dry Sugar Pack:* Pack dry whole fruit with the stated quantity of sugar: 100–150 g (4–6 oz) to 450 g (1 lb) fruit. Mix together. Pack in rigid containers.
Blackberries	Dry pack or dry sugar pack—allow 225 g (8 oz) sugar to 900 g (2 lb) fruit. Pack in rigid containers.
Blueberries or Bilberries	Wash in chilled water and drain thoroughly. Use one of the following methods: (a) Dry pack. (b) Dry sugar pack—about 100 g (4 oz) sugar to 450–700 g (1–1½ lb) fruit; slightly crush berries, mix with sugar until dissolved and then pack in rigid containers. (c) Cold syrup pack—900 g (2 lb) sugar dissolved in 1 litre (2 pints) water.
Gooseberries	Wash and dry thoroughly. Use one of the following methods: (a) Dry pack in polythene bags; use for pie fillings. (b) Cold syrup pack—900 g (2 lb) sugar to 1 litre (2 pints) water. (c) Purée—stew fruit in a very little water, rub through a nylon sieve and sweeten to taste; useful for fools and mousses.
Loganberries	Choose firm, clean fruit. Remove stalks. Dry pack in rigid containers or dry sugar pack—see Blackberries.
Strawberries and Raspberries	Choose firm, clean, dry fruit; remove hulls. Raspberries freeze well. Whole strawberries can be a disappointment. Add a little lemon juice to strawberry purée. Use one of the following methods: (a) Dry pack. (b) Dry sugar pack—100 g (4 oz) sugar to each 450 g (1 lb) fruit. (c) Purée; sweeten to taste—about 50 g (2 oz) sugar per 225 g (8 oz) purée. Freeze in small containers; useful for ice creams, sorbets, sauces and mousses.
Blackcurrants	Wash, dry, top and tail. (a) Dry pack for whole fruit. (b) Purée—cook to a purée with very little water and brown sugar, according to taste.
Redcurrants	Wash and dry whole fruit, then dry pack in rigid containers.

Preparing Fruit for Freezing continued

Fruit	Preparation
Cherries	Remove the stalks, wash and dry. Use one of the following methods: (a) Dry pack. (b) Dry sugar pack—225 g (8 oz) sugar to 900 g (2 lb) stoned cherries. Pack in containers cooked or uncooked; best used stewed for pie fillings. (c) Cold syrup pack—450 g (1 lb) sugar to 1 litre (2 pints) water, mixed with 2.5 ml (1/2 tsp) ascorbic acid per 1 litre (2 pints) syrup; leave headspace. Do not open pack until required, as fruit loses colour rapidly on exposure to air.
Damsons	Wash in cold water. The skins are inclined to toughen during freezing. Use one of the following methods: (a) Purée. (b) Halve, remove the stones and pack in cold syrup—450 g (1 lb) sugar to 1 litre (2 pints) water. They will need cooking after freezing; can be used as stewed fruit. (c) Poach and sweeten.
Figs	Wash gently to avoid bruising, then remove stems. Use one of the following methods: (a) Freeze unsweetened, either whole or peeled, in polythene bags. (b) Peel and pack in cold syrup—450 g (1 lb) sugar to 1 litre (2 pints) water. (c) Leave whole and wrap in foil; suitable for dessert figs.
Grapefruit	Peel fruit, removing all pith, then segment. Use one of the following methods: (a) Cold syrup pack—equal quantities of sugar and water (use any juice from the fruit to make up the syrup). (b) Dry sugar pack—225 g (8 oz) sugar to 450 g (1 lb) fruit, sprinkled over fruit; when juices start to run, pack in rigid containers.
Grapes	The seedless variety can be packed whole; others should be skinned, pipped and halved. Pack in cold syrup—450 g (1 lb) sugar to 1 litre (2 pints) water.
Greengages	Wash in cold water, halve, remove stones. Pack in cold syrup—450 g (1 lb) sugar to 1 litre (2 pints) water, with the juice of 1 lemon added. Place in rigid containers. Do not open pack until required, as fruit loses colour rapidly. Skins tend to toughen during freezing.
Lemons and Limes	Use one of the following methods: (a) Squeeze out juice and freeze it in ice-cube trays; remove frozen cubes to polythene bags for storage. (b) Leave whole, slice or segment before freezing. (c) Remove all pith from the peel, cut into julienne strips, blanch for 1 minute, cool and pack; use for garnishing dishes. (d) Mix grated lemon peel and a little sugar to serve with pancakes. (e) Remove slivers of peel, free of pith, and freeze in foil packs to add to drinks.
Mangoes	Peel and slice ripe fruit. Pack in cold syrup—450 g (1 lb) sugar to 1 litre (2 pints) water; add 30 ml (2 tbsp) lemon juice to each 1 litre (2 pints) syrup. Serve with additional lemon juice.
Melons	Cantaloup and honeydew melons freeze quite well (though they lose their crispness when thawed), but the seeds of watermelon make it more difficult to prepare. (a) Cut in half and seed, then cut flesh into balls, cubes or slices. Pack immediately in cold syrup—450 g (1 lb) sugar to 1 litre (2 pints) water. (b) Dry pack, with a little sugar sprinkled over. Pack in polythene bags.

Preparing Fruit for Freezing continued

Fruit	Preparation
Oranges	Prepare and pack as for grapefruit, or use one of the following methods: (a) Squeeze out and freeze the juice; add sugar if desired and freeze in small quantities in containers or in ice-cube trays. (b) Grate peel for orange sugar as for lemon sugar. (c) Seville oranges may be scrubbed, packed in suitable quantities and frozen whole until required for making marmalade. (Do not thaw whole frozen fruit in order to cut it up before cooking as some discoloration often occurs—use whole fruit method for marmalade. It is advisable to add one-eighth extra weight of Seville or bitter oranges or tangerines when freezing for subsequent marmalade making in order to offset pectin loss.)
Peaches	Skin and stone really ripe peaches under running water, as scalding will soften and slightly discolour the flesh. Treat firm peaches in the usual way. Brush over with lemon juice. (a) Pack halves or slices in cold syrup—450 g (1 lb) sugar to 1 litre (2 pints) water, with the juice of 1 lemon added; pack in rigid containers, leaving 1 cm (½ inch) headspace. (b) Purée peeled and stoned peaches. Mix in 15 ml (1 tbsp) lemon juice and 100 g (4 oz) sugar to each 450 g (1 lb) fruit; suitable for sorbets and soufflé-type desserts.
Pears	It is really only worthwhile freezing pears if you have a large crop from your garden, as they discolour rapidly, and the texture of thawed pears can be unattractively soft. Peel, quarter, remove core and dip in lemon juice immediately. Poach in syrup—450 g (1 lb) sugar to 1 litre (2 pints) water—for 1½ minutes. Drain, cool and pack in the cold syrup.
Pineapple	Only freeze quality ripe fruit. Peel and core, then slice, dice, crush or cut into wedges. Use one of the following methods: (a) Pack unsweetened in rigid containers, separated by non-stick paper. (b) Cold syrup pack—450 g (1 lb) sugar to 1 litre (2 pints) water— in rigid containers; include any pineapple juice from the preparation. (c) Pack crushed pineapple in rigid containers, allowing 100 g (4 oz) sugar to about 350 g (12 oz) fruit.
Plums	Wash, halve and discard stones. Pack in cold syrup—use 450 g (1 lb) sugar to 1 litre (2 pints) water with the juice of 1 lemon—in rigid containers. Do not open pack until required, as fruit loses colour rapidly.
Rhubarb	Wash, trim and cut into 1–2.5 cm (½–1 inch) lengths. Heat in boiling water for 1 minute and cool quickly. Pack in cold syrup, using equal quantities sugar and water, or dry pack; use for pies and crumbles.

Fruits not suitable for freezing: Bananas, pomegranates.

FREEZING MEAT

Ready-butchered meat needs very little preparation before freezing. Excess fat should be removed as it tends to go rancid more quickly than the flesh during storage. Wherever possible, it is a good idea to remove any bones as well—they take up valuable space without giving any return for your money. It is better to make stock or soup with the bones and freeze that instead, therefore using up much less freezer space.

It saves space if you freeze stock rather than bones.

It is essential to package meat well, excluding as much air as possible to prevent the fat going rancid and the meat drying out. Use heavy duty polythene bags. Group in similar types, and overwrap with mutton cloth, stockinette, thin polythene or newspaper, to protect against puncturing and loss of quality. Separate chops and steaks with layers of greaseproof or non-stick paper.

Freezing Bacon

Only very fresh bacon should be frozen; the longer bacon has been cut or kept in the shop, the shorter its storage life in the freezer.

Commercial vacuum-packed bacon is good for freezing as the maximum amount of air has already been extracted from the inside the wrapping. Alternatively, freeze top quality bacon, closely wrapped in freezer wrap or foil and overwrapped in polythene bags. If wished, rashers can be interleaved with waxed or non-stick paper. Wrap bacon chops individually in foil, then pack together in a polythene bag. Joints up to 1.5–2 kg (3–4 lb) should be wrapped in foil, and then over-wrapped in a polythene bag.

FREEZING POULTRY AND GAME

It is only worth freezing young, plump, tender birds. Commercially frozen raw poultry is so readily available it is only an advantage to freeze poultry at home when the price is very favourable.

Turn the freezer temperature control down low at least 24 hours before planning to freeze a bird—you need to freeze it at the lowest possible temperature for your freezer—ideally $-32°C$ ($-26°F$). Once the chicken is frozen, return to the normal freezer temperature.

Whole Birds

After plucking and drawing, wipe the bird. Do not stuff the chicken, as it takes too long to freeze and thaw; freeze any stuffing separately. Pack the giblets separately because they will only keep for a quarter of the time the chicken can be stored.

To truss the bird, place it on the table with the breast uppermost. Insert the trussing needle, threaded with fine string, through the top joint of one leg, through the body and out through the other leg, leaving an end of string. Catch in the wing, then pass the needle through the body and catch in the bottom of the opposite leg. Again, insert the needle through the bottom end of the leg, pass the needle through the body and through the bottom of the opposite leg. Finally, pass the needle diagonally through the body and catch in the remaining wing. Tie the string tightly and securely.

To truss the bird without using a special needle, insert a skewer through the body just below the thigh bone and turn the chicken over on its breast. Catching in the wing tips, pass the string under the ends of the skewer and cross it over the back. Turn

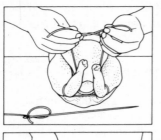

Trussing the legs of a chicken.

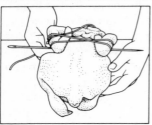

Using a trussing needle to truss a chicken.

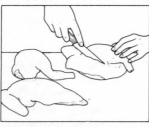

Dividing poultry into portions.

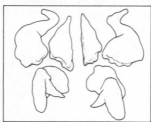

Poultry divided into six portions.

the bird over and tie the ends of the string round the tail, at the same time securing the drumsticks.

Portions

Divide small birds, around 1–1.4 kg (2–3 lb), into quarters, using poultry shears or a sharp knife. Cut the bird in half, through and along the breastbone. Open the bird out, then cut along the length of the backbone, using a knife or poultry shears.

If you want to remove the backbone entirely, cut along either side of it, then lift out. If you are using a knife, you will have to tap the back sharply with a heavy weight to cut through the bony sections. Once the bird is in two halves, lay them skin side up and divide each in half again by cutting diagonally across between wing and thigh—allocating more breast meat to the wing than to the thigh, to even out the amount of meat per portion.

Smaller Chicken Joints

For smaller joints for casseroles, use a larger bird. Cut the thigh loose along the rounded edge and pull the leg away from the body to dislocate the joint. Break the thigh backwards so that the knife can cut through the socket of each thigh joint, and loosen the wings from the breast meat in the same way. Divide the legs into two pieces in the centre of the joint. Turn over the body of the bird on its back and carve the breast meat from the breastbone. Both breast portions may be halved, and the back divided into two or three pieces or used to supplement the stock pot.

Packing Poultry

Before packing whole birds in freezer bags, first pad the legs with foil so that they cannot spike their way through the wrapping. Exclude as much air as possible before sealing the bag.

With chicken quarters or joints, pack individually in foil or polythene bags, then combine into a larger package.

Cold roast or poached chicken should be cooled as rapidly as possible after cooking. Parcel small amounts in foil, with any stuffing packed separately, and freeze at once.

Turkeys

In general, these are treated like chickens. But because they are so bulky, they take up a lot of valuable freezer space, so it is not good planning to store them for too long.

Leftover roast turkey may be frozen as

for chicken. It is best cut off the bone, and any fat should be discarded, while stuffing should be packed separately. To avoid excessive drying, freeze it with gravy or stock, unless only storing for a very short time.

Ducklings and Geese
Choose young birds without too much fat, which can cause rancidity—although excessively lean birds may be dry. Dress in the usual way, packing the giblets separately. Freeze as for chicken.

Hares (including Rabbits)
Prepare as for cooking fresh. If you like the gamey flavour, hang a hare for 5–7 days before freezing. Rabbits are not hung.

Since most recipes call for portioned hare or rabbit, it is sensible to pack them this way, discarding the more bony parts (which can be used for casseroles, pâté and stock). Pack and freeze as for meat.

Game Birds
These actually improve with freezing. Bleed the bird as soon as possible after shooting. Hang, undrawn, until sufficiently 'high' for your personal taste. Five–six days is long enough before freezing. If necessary, a bird can be frozen for a short time with its feathers on, and plucked after thawing.

Pluck, removing the feathers in the direction in which they grow. Draw, wash, drain and thoroughly dry. Pack, removing as much air as possible, in a really heavy-gauge foil or freezer bag before freezing in the usual way.

Water Birds
These should be plucked, drawn and frozen quickly after killing. (Remove the oil sac from the base of the tail.)

FREEZING FISH AND SHELLFISH

Fish for freezing must be really fresh—it should be frozen within 12 hours of being caught. Wash, then remove the scale, scrape tail-to-head with the back of a knife.

To gut round fish, make a slit along the abdomen from the gills to the tail vent and remove the insides. Clean away any blood by rubbing with a little salt to remove the black skin and blood. Rinse under cold running water. Drain and pat dry with absorbent kitchen paper.

To gut flat fish, open the cavity which lies in the upper part of the body under the gills and clean out the entrails in the same way. Rinse under cold running water. Drain and dry with absorbent kitchen paper.

To freeze a whole fish, for best results, place the fish unwrapped in the freezer until solid. Remove and dip in cold water: this will form a layer of thin ice over the fish and is known as 'ice glazing'. Return the fish to the freezer and repeat the process until the ice glaze is 0.5 cm (¼ inch) thick. Wrap in freezer wrap and support with a thin board.

To freeze fish steaks, separate them with a double layer of freezer wrap, then overwrap in foil or freezer wrap.

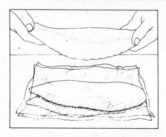

Interleave fish fillets with plastic wrap for freezing.

Shellfish should only be frozen if you can freeze them within 12 hours of being caught.

Cooked fish, in pies, fish cakes, croquettes, kedgeree or paella, should be prepared according to the recipe, but be absolutely sure the fish is very fresh. (See also page 36.)

Freezing Dairy Products

Butter and Margarine
Always buy fresh stock (farmhouse butter must be made from pasteurised cream).

Overwrap in foil in 225–450 g ($^1/_2$–1 lb) quantities.

Eggs
Freeze only fresh eggs out of their shells—yolks and whites separately. Pack in rigid containers. Yolks—to every 6 yolks add 5 ml (1 tsp) salt or 10 ml (2 tsp) sugar; to single yolks add 2.5 ml ($^1/_2$ tsp) salt or sugar.

Milk
Ordinary pasteurised milk does not freeze well. Homogenised is satisfactory. Pack in rigid containers; allow 2.5 cm (1 inch) headspace. *Do not freeze in the bottle.*

Yogurt
Fruit yogurts are satisfactory but natural yogurts do not freeze well. Some can be bought ready frozen. Freeze in retail cartons.

Cheese
Soft cheeses and full-fat cheeses are suitable for freezing. Hard cheeses become crumbly if stored for too long but are fine grated for cooking. Blue cheese also become crumbly. Cottage cheese not suitable for freezing. Wrap cheese in foil, then in a polythene bag.

Cream
Use only pasteurised, with a 35 per cent butterfat content or more, such as double or whipping cream. Whipped cream may be piped into rosettes on waxed paper. Best results are achieved with half-whipped cream with a little sugar added—5 ml (1 tsp) to 150 ml ($^1/_4$ pint).

Transfer cream to suitable container, such as a waxed carton, leaving headspace for expansion. Open freeze rosettes; when firm, pack in a single layer in foil.

STORING FOOD

If food is stored in a freezer at a constant temperature of − 18°C (0°F) it will keep almost indefinitely, however there will be some deterioration in the flavour, colour, texture and taste. Food is perfectly safe to eat after long periods of freezing because at this temperature food poisoning bacteria cannot multiply in or on the frozen food.

However, food contaminated before it is frozen will still be contaminated when thawed. If frozen food is allowed to thaw out and is kept at room temperature (unrefrigerated), bacteria will develop and the food will become a health hazard. This is because micro-organisms require a temperature above 7°C (45°F) to multiply.

Different foods have different storage times and these are determined by the length of time foods can be stored without any detectable change in eating quality.These are determined by the composition of the food, for example how much fat and water the food contains and whether the food is strongly flavoured.

Maximum recommended storage time for most vegetables is 10–12 months; for most fruits packed in syrup or sugar, 9–12 months; for fruits packed alone or as a purées 6–8 months; fruit juices, 4–6 months. Meats like beef can be stored for up to 8 months, but fattier meats like pork should preferable be kept for no longer than 6 months. This is because the fat tends to oxidise and go rancid, something that destroys fat-soluble vitamins such as vitamin A, as well as spoiling flavour. Oxidation can take place in oily fish like mackerel, too, which is why they can only be kept for 2 months, as opposed to 3 months for white fish.

Although the ideal is to store food at a constant temperature of − 18°C (0°F), every time you take something out of the freezer, the temperature is going to rise, and it is going to take some time for the thermostat-controlled compressor to bring it back to normal. Similarly, every time you add an unfrozen product, you are going to create a small temperature gradient— though you can keep it to the minimum by chilling packages in the refrigerator first.

These small fluctuations of temperature are fairly harmless. Big swings aren't, however, because even if you have quick-frozen your food, any pronounced fluctuation is still going to affect ice crystal formation—with possible loss of quality.

Really drastic rises in temperature excluded and presuming your food has been efficiently packaged, it shouldn't come to any real harm through faulty storage. Even if a temperature gradient has been set up, causing air to circulate and draw out more moisture than usual, your food will not be able to suffer desiccation or freezer burn if none of the air can reach it. In fact, the only scope for damage inside an airtight package is if you didn't manage to squeeze out all the air to begin with. Then, it is possible for air to circulate within the package, drying out the food and depositing the moisture on the insides of the pack as cavity ice—a process that cannot be put right at the thawing stage. All of which underlines just how vital the packaging stage is.

RECOMMENDED STORAGE TIMES

Meat

Beef: 8 months

Lamb: 6 months

Veal: 6 months

Pork: 6 months

Freshly minced meat: 3 months

Offal: 3 months

Cured and smoked meats: 1–2 months

Sausages: 3 months

Vacuum-packed bacon: 3 months

Smoked rashers, chops, gammon
    steaks and joints: 2 months

Unsmoked rashers, chops, gammon
    steaks and joints: 1 month

Poultry and Game

Chicken : 12 months

Duck: 4–5 months

Goose: 4–5 months

Turkey: 6 months

Giblets: 2–3 months

Game birds: 9 months

Water birds: 6 months

Venison: 12 months

Fish and Shellfish

White fish: 3 months

Oily fish including salmon: 2 months

Smoked salmon: 2–3 months

Caviar: do not freeze

Shellfish: 1 month

Vegetables

Vegetables: 10–12 months

Vegetable purées: 6–8 months

Fruit

Packed in syrup or sugar: 9–12 months

Packed alone or as a purée: 6–8 months

Fruit juices: 4–6 months

Dairy Foods

Butter, salted: 3 months

Butter, unsalted: 6 months

Margarine: as butter

Fresh shredded suet: 6 months

Milk: 1 month

Fresh double or whipping cream: 3
    months

Commercially frozen cream: up to 1 year

Eggs, separated: 8–10 months

Yogurt: 6 weeks

Cheese: 3–6 months

Note: See also A–Z Cooked Dishes and Baking on pages 36–42.

Right: Golden Vegetable Soup (page 54), Turkey Terrine (page 59) and Soda Bread (page 86)
Overleaf: Lemon Swiss Roll (page 94) and Almond and Cherry Flan (page 82)

THAWING FOOD

Some foods can be cooked or reheated straight from frozen, others need to thaw first. (See also Thawing Frozen Food in the Microwave on pages 43–47.)
Note: It is perfectly safe to cook thawed meat and then refreeze it, provided it is cooled quickly before freezing.
Once thawed, treat all foods as fresh and use as soon as possible.

MEAT

Meat can be thawed at cool room temperature, but there is less risk of contamination if it is thawed in the refrigerator. If the juices which have come from the meat during thawing are used in cooking they should be cooked as soon as possible.

The quickest way to thaw meat is to cook it from frozen. Boned and rolled cuts of meat should however not be cooked from frozen. Cooking times for frozen joints over 2.7 kg (6 lb) are very difficult to calculate. To prevent the outside being overcooked before the inside is thawed, it is better to thaw large joints before cooking.

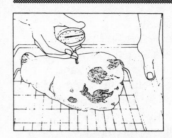

Testing a joint of meat with a thermometer.

To roast from frozen successfully, it is essential to use a meat thermometer. To test if cooked, shortly before the estimated cooking time, insert the thermometer into the centre of the meat or, if applicable, as near the bone as possible, making sure that the point of the thermometer does not touch the bone.

ROASTING MEAT FROM FROZEN

Meat joints on the bone	Approximate cooking time at 180°C (350°F) mark 4	Thermometer
Beef		
Under 1.8 kg (4 lb)	Well done—35 minutes per 450 g (1 lb) + 35 minutes.	79°C (170°F)
	Medium/rare—30 minutes per 450 g (1 lb) + 30 minutes.	71°C (160°F)
1.8–2.7 kg (4–6 lb)	Well done—40 minutes per 450 g (1 lb) + 40 minutes.	79°C (170°F)
	Medium/rare—35 minutes per 450 g (1 lb) + 35 minutes.	71°C (160°F)
Lamb		
Under 1.8 kg (4 lb)	Well done—35 minutes per 450 g (1 lb) + 35 minutes.	82°C (180°F)
1.8–2.7 kg (4–6 lb)	Well done—40 minutes per 450 g (1 lb) + 40 minutes.	
Pork		
1.8–2.7 kg (4–6 lb)	Well done—45 minutes per 450 g (1 lb) + 45 minutes.	88°C (190°C)

Note: Continue cooking until correct temperature is reached. If a roasting bag is used, reduce cooking time by 15 minutes per 450 g (1 lb).

Previous page: Chinese Pork and Ginger Casserole (page 67)
Left: Orange Sherbet (page 85), Rhubarb and Orange Fool (page 80) and Gingerbread Men (page 92)

Boned and Rolled Joints

Rolled joints such as breast of lamb, whether stuffed or not, must be thawed before cooking. This is because all the surfaces of the meat have been handled and rolled up, so it is important to ensure thorough cooking to destroy any bacteria which might be present in the meat.

Small Cuts of Meat

Chops, steaks, sausages, liver slices and kidneys can be easily cooked from frozen and so can cubed meat for stews and kebabs. Start the cooking at a lower temperature than normal and cook for almost twice as long, increasing the temperature half way through the cooking. It will probably be necessary to thaw meat for frying if it has become mis-shapen during freezing to ensure good contact with the frying pan.

Pot Roasting and Boiling

For the best results, it is advisable to thaw pot-roasting and boiling joints before cooking.

Stewing

Cubed and minced meat can be cooked from frozen. Allow extra time for cooking to allow for thawing.

Stews, pre-cooked pies and casseroles

These can be reheated from frozen, but unless you freeze them in fairly shallow dishes to begin with, there is always the danger they will not have reheated right through. Ideally thaw at cool room temperature.

Bacon

Must be thawed before cooking.

POULTRY

All frozen poultry must be completely thawed before cooking. If the giblets are inside the body cavity, remove them as soon as possible. The bird is completely thawed when no ice crystals remain in the body cavity and the limbs are flexible. It is then as perishable as fresh meat and should be cooked as soon as possible.

In the light of recent research, it is recommended that poultry is thawed in its wrapping at cool room temperature of 16–17°C (61–63°F) rather than in the refrigerator.

Remember to leave plenty of time for thawing poultry; a turkey can take a few days. If not cooked immediately, refrigerate until ready to roast.

FISH

To retain their juiciness and texture, whole fish are best thawed at cool room temperature before cooking, as are large portions for deep frying. Small fish and cuts such as fillets and steaks are best cooked from frozen.

VEGETABLES

These should be cooked from frozen. Try slow-cooking them in a heavy saucepan with a knob of butter or margarine instead of water, to preserve the vitamins. Blanching partially cooks the vegetables so they need shorter cooking times.

FRUIT

If the fruit is to be served without further preparation, thaw it slowly in the unopened container to prevent it from going too soft and mushy. Eat while still slightly chilled; turn it into a dish only just before serving. Fruits which tend to discolour, such as peaches, should be thawed more rapidly and kept submerged in the syrup while thawing. Allow 6–8 hours per 450g (1 1lb) fruit in the refrigerator or 2–4 hours at cool room temperature. Dry sugar packs thaw rather more quickly than fruit in syrup. For quick thawing, place the container in slightly warm water for 30 minutes to 1 hour.

If the fruit is to be cooked, thaw it until the pieces are just loosened. Cook as for fresh fruit, but do not forget that it will already be sweet if it has been packed in dry sugar or syrup.

DAIRY FOODS

Thaw milk in the refrigerator. Thawing may be accelerated if milk is to be used in cooking.

Thaw yogurt for about 1 hour at cool room temperature.

Thaw cheese for 24 hours in the refrigerator and allow to come to room temperature before serving. Use grated cheese straight from frozen.

Allow butter or margarine to thaw at cool room temperature—4 hours for a 250 g (8.82 oz) block.

Thaw separated eggs in the refrigerator.

Thaw cream in the refrigerator, allowing 24 hours, or at cool room temperature. Put rosettes in position as decoration before thawing, or they are difficult to handle; these take much less time to thaw.

COOKING AND REHEATING FROM FROZEN

In general, foods that can be cooked or reheated from frozen should be heated as rapidly as possible, to preserve the flavour and texture. Whenever practical, heat from frozen. If you are using the oven you will find that a temperature of about 200° C (400° F) mark 6 will be fine for combined thawing and reheating from frozen.

As a guide, a shallow 1 litre (2 pint) pack will take about 1 hour. (The advantage of freezing in smallish packs is obvious when it comes to reheating.) You can speed up the process a little by leaving the item unlidded. A sauce, once thawed, should be vigorously whisked to restore its smoothness, unless this would break down any firm pieces.

If you have only a small amount of food to reheat, use a double boiler; if in a hurry, a mixture that includes some sauce or liquid, such as a stew or soup, can be put into a heavy-based saucepan placed directly over the heat, but beware of sticking.

A–Z Cooked Dishes and Baking

Meat and Fish Dishes

Food and storage time	Preparation	Freezing	Thawing and serving
Meat, Cooked Dishes Casseroles, stews, curries: 2–3 months	Prepare as recipe, see that the meat is cooked but not overcooked, to allow for reheating. Do not season too heavily—adjust this on serving. Have enough liquid or sauce to immerse solid meat completely. Potato, rice or spaghetti, unless otherwise stated, are best added when serving.	When mixture is cold, transfer to rigid containers; for dishes with a strong smell or colour, line cartons with polythene bags, use foil dishes or freeze in foil-lined cookware. See preforming, page 18.	Reheat food from containers or polythene bags in a saucepan or casserole. Pre-shaped foil-wrapped mixtures can be reheated in the original dish. When reheating in a casserole, allow at least 1 hour for heating through in the oven at 200°C (400°F) mark 6, then if necessary reduce heat to 180°C (350°F) mark 4, for 40 minutes and leave until really hot. Alternatively, heat gently in a heavy-based pan, simmering until thoroughly heated. Or thaw before reheating.
Meat, Roast Sliced with gravy: 3 months Without gravy: 2 months	Joints can be roasted and frozen for serving cold—don't overcook. Reheated whole joints are not very satisfactory. Sliced and frozen cooked meats tends to be dry when reheated.	Best results are achieved by freezing whole joint, thawing, then slicing prior to serving. But small pieces can be sliced and packed in polythene bags to serve cold, or put in foil containers and covered with gravy to serve hot.	Allow plenty of time for thawing—about 4 hours per 450 g (1 lb) at cool room temperature, or double that time in the refrigerator, in the wrapping. Sliced meat requires less time.
Meat Loaves, Pâtés 1 month	Prepare as recipe. Package in the usual way, after cooling rapidly. Keep for minimum time.	When cold, remove from tin, wrap and freeze.	Thaw, preferably overnight. A change in texture and flavour is sometimes noticeable.
Fish, Cooked Dishes Pies, fish cakes, croquettes, kedgeree, mousse, paellas: 1–2 months	Prepare as recipe, but be sure fish is absolutely fresh. Hard-boiled eggs should be added to kedgeree before reheating.	Freeze in foil-lined containers, remove when hard, then pack in sealed bags.	Either slow thaw in refrigerator or put straight into the oven at 180°C (350°F) mark 4, to heat, depending on recipe.

PASTRY, PANCAKES AND PIZZAS

Food and storage time	Preparation	Freezing	Thawing and serving
Pastry, Uncooked 3 months	Roll out to size required (or shape into vol-au-vent cases). Freeze pie cases unwrapped until hard, to avoid damage. Use foil plates or take frozen case out of dish after freezing but before wrapping. Rounds of pastry can be stacked with waxed paper between. *Note:* Blocks of shortcrust pastry takes about 3 hours to thaw before it can be rolled out. Bulk flaky and puff—prepare up to the last rolling; pack in polythene or foil. Overwrap.	Stack pastry shapes with 2 pieces of freezer wrap between layers, so that if needed, one piece can be removed without thawing the whole batch. Place the stack on a piece of cardboard, wrap and seal.	Thaw flat rounds at room temperature, fit into pie plate and proceed with recipe. Unbaked pie cases or flat cases should be returned to their original container before cooking: bake in the oven from the freezer (ovenproof glass should first stand for 10 minutes at room temperature); add about 5 minutes to normal baking time. For blocks of uncooked pastry, leave for 3–4 hours at cool room temperature, or overnight in refrigerator.
Pastry, Cooked 3 months	Prepare as usual. Empty cases freeze satisfactorily, but with some change in texture. Prepare pies as directed (using a foil dish). Brush pastry cases with egg white before filling. Cool completely before freezing.	Wrap carefully as very fragile. Protect the tops of pies with an inverted paper or foil pie plate, then wrap and seal.	Leave pies at cool room temperature for 2–4 hours, depending on size. If required hot, reheat in the oven. Flan cases should be thawed at cool room temperature for about 1 hour, refresh if wished.
Pastry Pies, **Uncooked** Double crust: 3 months	Prepare pastry and filling as required. Make large pies in a foil dish or plate, or line an ordinary dish or plate with foil and use as a preformer. Make small pies in patty tins or foil cases. Do not slit top crust of fruit pies.	Freeze uncovered. When frozen, remove small or preformed pies from containers and pack all pies in foil or polythene bags.	Unwrap unbaked fruit pies and place still frozen in the oven at 220°C (425°F) mark 7, for 40–60 minutes, according to type and size. Slit tops of double crusts when beginning to thaw. (Ovenproof glass should first stand for 10 minutes at room temperature.) Add a little to cooking time.
Top crust: 3 months	Prepare as usual. Cut fruit into fairly small pieces and blanch if necessary; toss with sugar; or use cold cooked savoury filling. Cover with pastry. Do not slit crust.	Use ovenproof glass or foil dishes. Wrap in foil or freezer wrap, protecting as for cooked pies.	Unwrap, place in a reheated oven and bake, allowing extra time. Cut a vent in the pastry when it begins to thaw.

Pastries, Pancakes and Pizzas continued

Food and storage time	Preparation	Freezing	Thawing and serving
Biscuit pie crust: 2 months	Shape in a sandwich tin or pie plate, lined with foil or waxed paper. Add filling if suitable.	Freeze until firm, then remove from tin in the foil wrapping and pack in a rigid container.	Filled: serve cold; thaw at cool room temperature for 6 hours.
Pancakes, Unfilled 2 months	Add 15 ml (1 tbsp) corn oil to a basic 100 g (4 oz) flour recipe. Make pancakes, and cool quickly on a wire rack. Interleave with lightly oiled non-stick paper or freezer wrap. Seal in polythene bags or foil.	Freeze quickly.	Leave in packaging at cool room temperature for 2–3 hours, or overnight in the refrigerator. For quick thawing, unwrap, spread out separately and leave at cool room temperature for about 20 minutes. To reheat, place stack of pancakes with foil in the oven at 190°C (375°F) mark 5, for 20–30 minutes. Alternatively, separate pancakes and place in a lightly greased heated frying pan, allowing ½ minute for each side.
Pancakes, Filled 1–2 months	Only choose fillings suitable for freezing. Do not over-season.	Place filled pancakes in a foil dish, seal and overwrap.	Place frozen, covered, in oven at 200°C (400°F) mark 6, for about 30 minutes.
Pizza, Unbaked Up to 3 months	Prepare traditional yeast mixture to baking stage. Wrap in foil or polythene.	Freeze flat until solid, then overwrap in ones, twos, threes or fours.	Remove packaging and place frozen in cold oven set at 230°C (450°F) mark 8, then bake for 30–35 minutes.
Pizza, Baked Up to 2 months	Bake traditional yeast mixture in usual way.	Package in foil or polythene and freeze as for unbaked pizza.	Remove packaging and place frozen in a preheated oven at 200°C (400°F) mark 6, for about 20 minutes or leave in packaging at room temperature for 2 hours before reheating as above for 10–15 minutes.

CAKES, BISCUITS AND BREADS

Food and storage time	Preparation	Freezing	Thawing and serving
Cakes, Cooked Including sponge flans, Swiss rolls and layer cakes: 3 months (iced cakes and gâteaux lose quality after 2 months; since aging improves fruit cakes, they may be kept longer)	Bake in usual way. Leave until cold on a wire rack. Swiss rolls are best rolled up in greaseproof paper, if frozen without a filling. Do not spread or layer with jam before freezing. Keep flavourings to a minimum and use spices lightly.	Wrap plain cakes layers separately, or together with freezer wrap or waxed paper between layers. Freeze iced cakes and gâteaux (whole or cut) unwrapped until icing has set, then wrap, seal and pack in rigid boxes to protect icing.	Iced cakes and gâteaux: unwrap before thawing, then the wrapping will not stick to the decoration when thawing. Cream cakes: may be sliced while frozen, for a better shape and quick thawing. Plain cakes: leave in package and thaw at cool room temperature. Un-iced layer cake and small cakes thaw in about 1–2 hours at cool room temperature: iced cakes and gâteaux take up to 4 hours.
Cake Mixtures, Uncooked 2 months	Whisked sponge mixtures do not freeze well uncooked. Put rich creamed mixtures into containers, or line the tin to be used later with greased foil, add cake mixture and freeze uncovered. When frozen, remove from tin, package in foil and overwrap.	Return to freezer.	Leave at cool room temperature for 2–3 hours, then fill tins to bake. Preformed cake mixtures can be returned to the original tin, without wrapping but still in foil lining. Place frozen in preheated oven and bake in usual way, but allow longer cooking time.
Scones and Teabreads 3 months	Bake in usual way.	Freeze in polythene bag in convenient units for serving.	Thaw teabreads in wrapping at cool room temperature for 2–3 hours. Tea scones: cook from frozen, wrapped in foil, at 200°C (400°F) mark 6, for 10 minutes. Girdle scones: thaw 1 hour. Drop scones: thaw 30 minutes or cover and bake for 10 minutes.

Cakes, Biscuits and Breads continued.

Food and storage time	Preparation	Freezing	Thawing and serving
Croissants and Danish Pastries Unbaked, in bulk: 6 weeks Baked: 4 weeks.	Unbaked: prepare to the stage when all the fat has been absorbed, but do not give the final rolling. Baked: bake as usual.	Unbaked: wrap in polythene bags and freeze at once. Baked: pack in rigid containers.	Leave in polythene bag, but unseal and re-tie loosely, allowing space for dough to rise. Preferably thaw overnight in a refrigerator, or leave for 5 hours at cool room temperature. Complete the final rolling and shaping, and bake. Baked: loosen wrapping and thaw as for unbaked.
Biscuits, Baked and Unbaked 3 months	Prepare in the usual way. Rich mixtures, with more than 100 g (4 oz) fat to 450 g (1 lb) flour, are the most satisfactory.	Either baked or unbaked, pack carefully. Wrap rolls of uncooked dough, or pipe soft mixtures into shapes, freeze and pack when firm. Allow cooked biscuits to cool before packing.	Thaw uncooked rolls of dough slightly; slice off required number of biscuits and bake. Shaped biscuits can be cooked direct from frozen: allow 7–10 minutes extra cooking time. Cooked biscuits may required crisping in warm oven.
Bread 2 weeks	Freshly baked bread, both bought and homemade, can be frozen. Crisp, crusty bread stores well up to 1 week, then the crust begins to 'shell off'.	Bought bread may be frozen in original wrapper for up to 1 week; for longer periods, seal in foil or polythene. Homemade bread: freeze in foil or polythene bags.	Leave to thaw in the sealed polythene bag or wrapper at cool room temperature 3–6 hours, or overnight in the refrigerator. Alternatively, leave foil-wrapped and crisp in oven at 200° C (400° F) mark 6, for about 45 minutes. Sliced bought bread can be toasted from frozen.
Bought Part-Baked Breads and Rolls 4 months	Freeze immediately after purchase.	Leave loaf in the bag. Pack rolls in heavy-duty polythene bags and seal.	To use, place frozen unwrapped loaf in oven at 220° C (425° F) mark 7, for about 40 minutes. Cool for 1–2 hours before cutting. Rolls: place frozen unwrapped in oven at 200° C (400° F) mark 6, for 15 minutes.

40

PUDDINGS AND DESSERTS

Food and storage time	Preparation	Freezing	Thawing and serving
Sponge Puddings, Uncooked 1 month	Make in the usual way. Use foil or polythene basins, or line ordinary basins with greased foil.	Seal basins tightly with foil, overwrap and freeze at once. To freeze pudding mixture in preformed foil, remove from basins when frozen, then overwrap. *Note:* Allow room at this stage for later rising.	Remove packaging, cover top with greased foil and place, frozen, to steam—900 ml (1½ pint) size takes about 2½ hours. Return preformed pudding mixture to its original basin.
Sponge Puddings, Cooked 3 months	Prepare and cook in the usual way. Cool thoroughly, cover with foil and overwrap.	Freeze quickly.	As above—a 900 ml (1½ pint) pudding takes about 45 minutes to thaw and reheat.
Ice Cream 3 months Commercially made: 1 month	Either homemade or bought ice creams and sorbets can be stored in the freezer.	Bought ice creams should be rewrapped in moistureproof bags before storing. Homemade ones should be frozen in moulds or rigid containers and overwrapped.	Put in refrigerator for short time to soften a little. Some 'soft' bought ice cream can be used from freezer, provided it is not kept in the coldest part. Warn children that ice lollipops and water ices eaten straight from the freezer are dangerous—they may burn the mouth.
Sweets Mousses, creams, etc. 2 months	Make as usual. Any dishes used in freezer must be freezerproof.	Freeze, unwrapped, in foil-lined container until firm, then remove container. Place sweet in polythene bag, seal and return to freezer.	Unwrap preformed mixtures and return to dish. Thaw in refrigerator for about 6 hours, or at cool room temperature for about 2 hours.

MISCELLANEOUS

Food and storage time	Preparation	Freezing	Thawing and serving
Commercially Frozen Foods Up to 3 months as a rule *Note:* The times quoted by the manufacturers are often less than those given for home frozen foods, because of the handling in distribution, before the foods can reach your own freezer.	No further preparation needed, except for ice cream, which should be overwrapped if it is to be kept for longer than 3 weeks.	Follow directions on packet.	Follow directions on packet.
Herbs Up to 6 months	Wash and trim if necessary. Dry thoroughly.	Freeze in small bunches in a rigid foil container or polythene bag. Alternatively, herbs, especially parsley, can be chopped before freezing.	Can be used immediately. Crumble while still frozen.
Sauces, Soups, Stocks Sauces, soups: 3 months Stock: 6 months	All are very useful as standbys in the freezer.	When cold, pour into rigid containers, leaving headspace. Seal well and freeze.	Either thaw for 1–2 hours at cool room temperature, or heat gently in a heavy-based pan until boiling.
Sandwiches 1–2 months	Most types may be frozen, but those filled with hard–boiled eggs, tomatoes, cucumber or bananas tend to go tasteless and soggy.	Wrap in foil, then in polythene bag.	Thaw unwrapped at cool room temperature or in the refrigerator. Times vary according to size of pack. Cut pin-wheels, sandwich loaves, etc., in portions when half thawed.

THAWING FROZEN FOOD IN THE MICROWAVE

Food can be thawed in the microwave in a fraction of the time it would take to thaw conventionally, but it is essential that it thaws gently and evenly. When food is thawed, the small ice crystals melt first and if thawing in the microwave is too rapid, parts of the food will start to cook before the areas of large ice crystals have thawed. It is best to thaw food on LOW or DEFROST. Some cookers have an AUTO DEFROST setting which thaws food automatically; see the manufacturer's instructions.

If your microwave does not have a LOW or DEFROST setting, you can thaw manually by turning off the cooker every 30 seconds and allowing the food to stand for 1½ minutes before turning the cooker on again for another 30 seconds. The number of microwaving and resting times will depend on the size and amount of food being thawed—the larger the item the longer the periods of heating and resting. Dense foods like joints of meat need a standing time of at least 15–20 minutes at the end of the thawing time.

Turn foods over during thawing and separate small items as soon as possible. Break up liquid or semi-liquid foods with a fork and shake or fork apart vegetables and small fruit. Stand foods such as breads, cakes and pastries on absorbent kitchen paper to absorb the moisture.

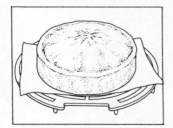

Stand foods such as breads, cakes and pastries on absorbent kitchen paper on a rack.

THAWING GUIDELINES

1 Always underestimate thawing times. Many foods will still be icy in the centre when removed from the microwave, but will melt through during the standing time. If necessary, food can be returned to the microwave for further thawing.

2 Remove metal twist ties from bags and replace with string or an elastic band before putting the bags in the microwave.

3 Remove all lids from jars or containers.

4 Open cartons and slit plastic pouches.

5 Only thaw food in the microwave if it is going to be cooked and eaten immediately.

6 If frozen food has to be placed in a dish, match the size and shape of dish to the size and shape of the food.

7 Food can be thawed in foil trays which do not exceed 2 cm (¾ inch) in depth.

8 For faster and more even thawing, separate frozen foods, such as chops and fish cutlets, into pieces as they thaw.

9 Turn food over if possible during thawing. If this is not possible, rearrange individual items or turn the dish round.

10 Shake or gently break down fruit during the thawing and standing time.

11 Flex pouches and packagings which cannot be broken up or stirred, to distribute the heat.

12 Pierce the skins of frozen foods such as frankfurters before thawing.

13 Pour off liquid from poultry which has been frozen and is being thawed in its original wrapping. This liquid absorbs microwave energy and slows down the thawing process.

14 Finish thawing poultry in cold water in its original closed polythene bag, rather than try to completely thaw it with

microwave energy, otherwise it may start to cook around the outside before it is fully thawed in the centre. Remember to remove giblets from thawed poultry before cooking.
15 Fish, seafood and meat can also be thawed in their original packages. These should be pierced or slit and any metal ties should be removed and replaced by string or an elastic band.
16 Cakes, bread and bread products, buns, scones, biscuits and pastry items should be placed on absorbent kitchen paper to absorb moisture during thawing.
17 Vegetables are best cooked directly from the freezer without being thawed.
18 If large items of food begin to thaw unevenly, small pieces of foil may be used to cover any areas which appear to be developing hot spots or beginning to cook.
19 Remember the thawing process will continue during the standing time. Do not attempt to completely thaw foods in a microwave, otherwise the outer edges will dry out, or even begin to cook.

THAWING GUIDE

Times are approximate and should be used only as a guide, since they may vary, depending not only on the shape, density and weight of frozen food, but also the temperature at which it was stored in the freezer. Refer to the manufacturer's instruction manual for specific times for your particular cooker.
Note: A 650 watt cooker was used for this thawing guide.

MEAT

Frozen meat exudes a lot of liquid during thawing and because microwaves are attracted to water, the liquid should be poured off or mopped up with absorbent kitchen paper when it collects, otherwise thawing will take longer. Start thawing a joint in its wrapper, first piercing it, and remove it as soon as possible—usually after one quarter of the thawing time. Place the joint on a microwave roasting rack.

Remember to turn over a large piece of meat. If the joint shows signs of cooking, give the meat a 'rest' period of 20 minutes. A joint is thawed when a skewer can easily pass through the thickest part of the meat. Chops and steaks should be re-positioned during thawing; test them by pressing the surface with your fingers—the meat should feel cold to the touch and give in the thickest part.

Food	Quantity	Weight or size	Approximate time on LOW or DEFROST	Further instructions
Beef boned roasting joints (sirloin, topside)		per 450 g (1 lb)	8–10 minutes	Turn over regularly during thawing and rest if the meat shows signs of cooking. Stand for 1 hour.
joints on bone (rib of beef)		per 450 g (1 lb)	10–12 minutes	Cover bone end with foil. Turn over during thawing. The meat will still be icy in the centre but to complete thawing stand for 1 hour.
minced beef		450 g (1 lb)	8–10 minutes	Stand for 10 minutes.
cubed steak		450 g (1 lb)	6–8 minutes	Stand for 10 minutes.
steak (sirloin, rump)		per 450 g (1 lb)	8–10 minutes	Stand for 10 minutes.
beefburgers standard	2 4	50 g (2 oz)	2 minutes 2–3 minutes	Can be cook from frozen without thawing, if preferred.

Meat continued

Food	Quantity	Weight or size	Approximate time on LOW or DEFROST	Further instructions
quarter-pounder	2	100 g	2–3 minutes	
	4	(4 oz)	5 minutes	
burger buns	2		2 minutes	Stand 2 minutes.
Lamb/Veal boned, rolled joints (loin, leg, shoulder)		per 450 g (1 lb)	5–6 minutes	As for boned roasting joints of beef.
joints on bone (leg, shoulder)		450 g (1 lb)	5–6 minutes	As for beef joints on the bone.
minced lamb or veal		450 g (1 lb)	8–10 minutes	Stand for 10 minutes.
lamb chops		450 g (1 lb)	8–10 minutes	Separate during thawing. Stand for 10 minutes.
Pork boned, rolled joint (loin, leg)		per 450 g (1 lb)	7–8 minutes	As for boned roasting joints of beef.
joints on bone (leg, hand)		per 450 g (1 lb)	7–8 minutes	As for beef joints on bone.
fillet or tenderloin		450 g (1 lb)	8–10 minutes	Stand for 10 minutes.
chops		450 g (1 lb)	8–10 minutes	Separate during thawing and arrange 'spoke' fashion. Stand for 10 minutes.
sausages		450 g (1 lb)	5–6 minutes	Separate during thawing. Stand for 10 minutes.
Offal liver		450 g (1 lb)	8–10 minutes	If sliced, separate during thawing. Stand for 5 minutes.
kidney		450 g (1 lb)	6–9 minutes	Separate during thawing. Stand for 5 minutes.
Bacon rashers	1 pack	225 g (8 oz)	2 minutes	Remove slices from pack and separate after thawing. Stand for 6–8 minutes.

POULTRY

Poultry should be thawed in its freezer wrapping, which should be pierced first and any metal tag removed. During thawing, pour off liquid that collects in the wrapping. Finish thawing in a bowl of cold water with the bird still in its wrapping. Chicken portions can be thawed in their polystyrene trays if shop-bought.

whole chicken or duckling	1	per 450 g (1 lb)	6–8 minutes	Remove giblets if necessary. Stand bird in cold water for 30 minutes.
whole turkey	1	per 450 g (1 lb)	10–18 minutes	Remove giblets if necessary. Stand bird in cold water for 2–3 hours.

Poultry continued

Food	Quantity	Weight or size	Approximate time on *LOW* or *DEFROST*	Further instructions
chicken portions		450 g (1 lb)	5–7 minutes	Separate during thawing. Stand for 10 minutes.
FISH white fish fillets or cutlets, eg cod, coley, haddock, halibut whole plaice or sole		450 g (1 lb)	3–4 minutes plus 2–3 minutes	Stand for 5 minutes between times and for 5 minutes afterwards. Separate during thawing. Finish thawing whole plaice or sole in cold water for 30 minutes to prevent drying out of the surface.
oily fish, eg mackerel, herring, trout, whole and gutted		225 g (8 oz)	2–3 minutes plus 3–4 minutes	Stand for 5 minutes between times and for 5 minutes afterwards.
kipper fillets		225 g (8 oz)	2–3 minutes	
lobster tails		225 g (8 oz)	3–4 minutes plus 2–3 minutes	Stand for 5 minutes between times and for 5 minutes afterwards.
prawns, shrimps, scampi, crabmeat	1 block	450 g (1 lb)	2–3 minutes plus 2–3 minutes	Stand for 5 minutes between times and for 5 minutes afterwards.
prawns		100 g (4 oz)	2½ minutes	Pierce polythene bag if necessary. Stand for 2 minutes. Stir, then separate with a fork. Cover with absorbent kitchen paper and stand for 3 minutes. Plunge into cold water and drain.
prawns		225 g (8 oz)	3–4 minutes	
RICE cooked		225 g (8 oz)	2 minutes	Break up with a fork after 1 minute.
VEGETABLES These can be cooked from frozen.				
BREAD loaf, whole loaf, whole	1 1	large small	6–8 minutes 4–6 minutes	Uncover and place in cooker on absorbent kitchen paper. Turn over during thawing. Stand for 5–15 minutes.
loaf, sliced loaf, sliced	1 1	large small	6–8 minutes 4–6 minutes	Defrost in original wrapper but remove any metal tags. Stand for 10–15 minutes.
slice of bread	1	25 g (1 oz)	10–15 seconds	Place on absorbent kitchen paper. Time carefully. Stand for 1–2 minutes.
bread rolls	2 4	— —	15–20 seconds 25–35 seconds	Place on absorbent kitchen paper. Time carefully. Stand for 2–3 minutes.
crumpets	2	—	15–20 seconds	As above
PASTRY shortcrust and puff	1 pack	227 g (8 oz)	1 minute	Stand for 20 minutes.
	1 pack	395 g (14 oz)	2 minutes	Stand for 20–30 minutes.

Cakes

Food	Quantity	Weight or size	Approximate time on LOW or DEFROST	Further instructions
CAKES	2	small	30–60 seconds	Place on absorbent kitchen paper.
cakes	4	small	1–1½ minutes	Stand for 5 minutes.
sponge cake	1	450 g (1 lb)	1–1½ minutes	Place on absorbent kitchen paper. Test and turn after 1 minute. Stand for 5 minutes.
cream sponge	1	15 cm (6 in) diameter	30 seconds on HIGH	Place on absorbent kitchen paper. Stand for 20–30 minutes.
jam doughnuts	2	—	45–60 seconds	Place on absorbent kitchen paper.
	4	—	45–90 seconds	Do not eat immediately as the jam will be very hot. Stand for 5 minutes.
cream doughnuts	2	—	45–60 seconds	Place on absorbent kitchen paper.
	4	—	1¼–1¾ minutes	Check after half the thawing time. Stand for 10 minutes.
cream éclairs	2	—	45 seconds	Stand for 5–10 minutes.
	4	—	1–1½ minutes	Stand for 15–20 minutes.
choux buns	4	small	1–1½ minutes	Stand for 20–30 minutes.
DAIRY PRODUCTS butter or margarine	1 pack	250 g (8.82 oz)	1½–2 minutes	Remove foil wrapping if necessary and place block on absorbent kitchen paper. Stand for 5 minutes.
cream, whipped		300 ml (½ pint)	1–2 minutes	Remove metal lid if necessary. Stand for 10–15 minutes.
full fat soft cheese		75 g (3 oz)	1–1½ minutes	Remove foil wrapping. Place on absorbent kitchen paper. Stand for 10–15 minutes.
DESSERTS cheesecake with fruit topping	1	about 23 cm (9 in) diameter	3–4 minutes	Place on serving dish. Stand for 20 minutes.
fruit pie	1	650 g (26 oz)	4–5 minutes	Stand for 5–10 minutes.
mousse	1	individual	30 seconds	Remove lid before thawing. Stand for 15–20 minutes.
trifles and melbas	1	individual	45–60 seconds	Remove lid before thawing. Stand for 15–20 seconds.
FRUIT soft fruit, eg strawberries, raspberries		225 g (8 oz)	3–5 minutes	Leave to stand until completely thawed. Stir gently during thawing and standing time.
		450 g (1 lb)	6–8 minutes	
fruit juice concentrate	1 can	178 ml (6¼ oz)	2–3 minutes	Remove the collar and lid. Stand for 3–5 minutes.

REHEATING FOOD IN THE MICROWAVE

The majority of foods can be reheated in the microwave without loss of quality, colour or flavour.

Reheating Guidelines

1 Place food in a shallow container so that the microwaves can penetrate the food easily. Do not use such a large dish that the sauce spreads thinly and burns.

2 Ensure that food is initially too hot to eat. If in any doubt, return to the microwave for a little longer. A useful test is to touch the base of the cooking dish after taking it out of the oven, if the centre is cold, so is the food.

3 Main course and meat dishes benefit from more gentle heating on low rather than high settings, especially if they have been refrigerated. Cover tightly during reheating.

4 Stir casseroles and main dishes if possible during reheating, to distribute heat and shorten the reheating period.

5 Dishes which cannot be stirred should be shaken gently and rotated manually.

6 Thin slices of meat will heat more evenly than thickly cut slices. Add sauce or gravy to provide moisture and prevent the meat from drying during reheating.

7 Do not reheat large pieces of meat, poultry or fish; if they are hot in the centre, the edges will overcook.

8 If you want to serve food on to a plate to reheat later, arrange it in an even layer, placing dense foods towards the outside of the plate and quicker heating foods in the centre. Cover plate with a lid to retain heat and moisture.

9 Vegetables in sauce reheat well in a covered dish. They should be stirred during reheating if possible, otherwise rotate the dish especially in cookers without a turntable.

10 Care is needed when reheating some vegetables with sauce, to prevent overcooking. Fibrous vegetables such as broccoli spears and asparagus tend to lose texture and toughen when reheated.

11 Wrap bread and bread products in absorbent kitchen paper to absorb moisture and do not overheat, otherwise they will toughen. One bread roll will be warm in about 10 seconds, and two will only need 10 to 15 seconds.

12 Cooked pastry items should be placed on absorbent kitchen paper to absorb moisture during reheating. Remember such foods heat extremely quickly in the microwave, especially if they have a sweet filling, such as fruit pies. The outer pastry will feel barely warm, but the filling will be very hot—the heat will equalise during a few minutes standing time. One mince pie will be heated in about 10 seconds. The microwave should not be left unattended during these short reheating periods.

13 Rice and pasta reheat beautifully. Add a little liquid or butter cover the dish and stir during reheating.

14 Exercise care when reheating starchy vegetables such as jacket potatoes to prevent overcooking or dehydration.

15 Refrigerated and frozen food will take longer to reheat than food at room temperature, frozen food requiring the longest time.

Blanching in the Microwave

Vegetables can be blanched very successfully in the microwave and in much smaller amounts of water. Small quantities of vegetables blanch more evenly than large—if necessary blanch in batches, microwaving the first batch while preparing the next batch. A 2 litre ($3^{1}/_{2}$ pint) casserole is suitable for most vegetables.

FREEZER RECIPES

STOCKS AND SOUPS

BEEF STOCK

Browning the bones in the oven before use gives this stock a good colour

MAKES 1.4 LITRES (2¹/₂ PINTS)
1.4–1.8 kg (3–4 lb) beef and veal bones
2 onions, skinned and quartered
2 carrots, peeled and quartered
2 celery sticks, sliced
bay leaf, parsley stalks, thyme sprigs, for flavouring
6–8 black peppercorns
salt

1 Place the bones in a roasting tin with the vegetables. Brown in the oven at 220°C (425°F) mark 7 for about 30–40 minutes. Turn the bones and vegetables occasionally.
2 Transfer the ingredients to a large saucepan. Add enough cold water to cover. Bring to the boil and skim. Add all the flavouring ingredients, except the salt.
3 Partially cover the pan and simmer very gently, skimming occasionally, for about 2–3 hours or until the liquid has reduced by one third.
4 Strain the stock, adjust seasoning, then cool. Skim off the fat before use.

CHICKEN STOCK

Leave this stock in the refrigerator overnight to set the fat for easy removal

MAKES 1.7 LITRES (3 PINTS)
1 chicken carcass plus bones, scraps of flesh and giblets (excluding liver), or about 700g (1¹/₂ lb) veal bones plus scraps of flesh
2 carrots, peeled and quartered
2 onions, skinned and quartered
2 celery sticks, sliced
bay leaf, parsley stalks, thyme sprigs, for flavouring
6–8 black peppercorns
salt

1 Place the chicken bones, flesh and giblets in a large saucepan. Cover with cold water, about 2.8 litres (5 pints), then bring to the boil. Skim any scum.
2 Add the vegetables and all the remaining ingredients, except the salt, to the pan. Bring to the boil again, skim and reduce the heat.
3 Partially cover the pan and simmer very gently for about 2–3 hours, skimming as necessary at frequent intervals, or until the liquid has reduced by about one third.
4 Strain the stock, adjust seasoning, then cool. Remove the fat before use.

To Freeze Stocks
Cool, then pack in useable quantities in polythene bag lined containers. Freeze until solid, then lift out of the containers. Freeze for up to 6 months.

To Thaw Stocks
Thaw overnight in the refrigerator and reheat in a saucepan. Or gently reheat from frozen in a bowl over a pan of boiling water, stirring as the block thaws. Alternatively, transfer the solid block to a medium bowl. Microwave on HIGH for about 3–4 minutes for 300 ml (¹/₂ pint), breaking up the block as it thaws.

FISH STOCK

The bones of sole make particularly good stock, so ask your fishmonger to save ones removed when filleting

MAKES ABOUT 1.1 LITRES (2 PINTS)
about 225 g (8 oz) clean fish bones (3–4 backbones)
1 onion, skinned and quartered
1 carrot, peeled and quartered
1 celery stick, sliced
bay leaf, parsley stalks, thyme sprigs, for flavouring
4–6 black peppercorns
salt

1 Rinse the bones and discard any heads and dark skin. Place all the ingredients, except the salt, in the saucepan. Add cold water to cover.
2 Bring to the boil and skim any scum from the surface. Simmer very gently for 20–30 minutes.
3 Strain the stock, then cool. Adjust seasoning.

Note: Do not simmer the stock for more than 30 minutes – the bones will begin to give the stock a bitter flavour. However, once the stock has been strained, it can be boiled down again to reduce.

WATERCRESS SOUP

The clean, tangy taste of this soup is ideal before a rich main course

SERVES 4
100 g (4 oz) butter
1 medium onion, skinned and chopped
2 bunches watercress
50 g (2 oz) plain flour
750 ml (1¼ pints) chicken or veal stock
300 ml (½ pint) milk
salt and pepper

1 Melt the butter in a saucepan, add the onion and cook gently for 10 minutes until soft but not coloured.
2 Meanwhile, wash and trim the watercress, leaving some of the stem, then chop roughly. Add the chopped watercress to the onion, cover the pan and cook gently for a further 4 minutes.
3 Add the flour and cook gently, stirring, for 1–2 minutes. Remove from the heat and gradually blend in the stock and milk. Bring to the boil, stirring constantly, then simmer for 3 minutes. Add salt and pepper to taste.
4 Sieve or purée the soup in a blender or food processor. Return to the rinsed-out pan and reheat gently, without boiling. Taste and adjust seasoning, if necessary. Serve hot.

To Freeze
Cool after puréeing, then pack into rigid containers, leaving headspace. Freeze for up to 3 months.

To Thaw and Serve
Reheat from frozen in a heavy-based saucepan.

CHICKEN AND PASTA BROTH

SERVES 4–6

two 275 g (10 oz) chicken portions
1–2 small leeks, trimmed, sliced and washed
2 carrots, peeled and thinly sliced
900 ml (1½ pints) chicken stock
1 bouquet garni
salt and pepper
50 g (2 oz) small pasta shapes
60 ml (4 tbsp) chopped fresh parsley

1 Put the chicken portions in a large saucepan. Add the leeks and carrots, then pour in the stock and 900 ml (1½ pints) water. Bring to the boil.
2 Add the bouquet garni and salt and pepper to taste, then lower the heat, cover and simmer for 30 minutes until the chicken is tender. Remove the chicken from the liquid and leave until cool enough to handle.
3 Meanwhile, add the pasta to the pan, bring back to the boil and simmer for about 12 minutes, stirring occasionally, until tender.
4 Remove the chicken from the bones and cut the flesh into bite-sized pieces, discarding all skin. Return to the pan and heat through. Discard the bouquet garni, adjust seasoning and add parsley.

To Freeze
Cook the pasta for only 10 minutes before combining with the chicken and vegetable broth. Cool, then pack without the bouquet garni or parsley into rigid containers, leaving headspace. Freeze for up to 3 months.

To Thaw and Serve
Reheat from frozen in a heavy-based saucepan, stirring until thawed. Increase heat and simmer gently for 5 minutes. Adjust seasoning and add parsley.

VICHYSOISSE
This velvety soup makes an elegant first course for summer dinner parties

SERVES 4

50 g (2 oz) butter
4 leeks, trimmed, sliced and washed
1 onion, skinned and sliced
1 litre (1¾ pints) chicken stock
2 potatoes, peeled and thinly sliced
salt and pepper
200 ml (7 fl oz) single cream
snipped chives, to garnish

1 Melt the butter in a heavy-based saucepan, add the leeks and onion and cook gently for about 10 minutes until soft but not coloured.
2 Add the stock and potatoes, then bring to the boil. Lower the heat, add salt and pepper to taste, cover and simmer for about 30 minutes until the vegetables are completely soft.
3 Sieve or purée the soup in a blender or food processor. Pour into a large serving bowl and stir in the cream. Taste and adjust seasoning if necessary. Chill for at least 4 hours. Sprinkle with chives just before serving.

To Freeze
Cool the puréed soup, then pack without the cream into rigid containers, leaving headspace. Freeze for up to 6 months.

To Thaw and Serve
Thaw overnight in the refrigerator. Whisk in the cream and adjust the seasoning, then chill until ready to serve.

FRENCH ONION SOUP

SERVES 4

50 g (2 oz) butter

15 ml (1 tbsp) vegetable oil

450 g (1 lb) onions, skinned and finely sliced

2.5 ml (½ tsp) sugar

salt and pepper

15 ml (1 tbsp) plain flour

1 litre (1¾ pints) beef stock

150 ml (¼ pint) dry white wine

75 g (3 oz) Gruyère cheese, grated

4 slices French bread, toasted on both sides

45 ml (3 tbsp) brandy

1 Melt the butter with the oil in a large, heavy-based saucepan. Add the onions, stir well, cover and cook gently, stirring occasionally, for 20 minutes.

2 When the onions are completely soft, add the sugar and a pinch of salt and increase the heat to high. Cook for about 2 minutes until the onions caramelise slightly. Stir in the flour and cook for 1 minute until light brown.

3 Stir in the stock and wine, add pepper to taste and bring to the boil. Half cover and simmer for 40 minutes.

4 Pile a little grated Gruyère on to each round of toasted bread and brown lightly under a preheated grill.

5 Add the brandy to the soup. Stir well, then taste and adjust seasoning. Pour into warmed soup bowls and float the pieces of toasted bread on top. Serve immediately.

To Freeze
Cool quickly at the end of step 3, then pack into rigid containers, leaving headspace. Freeze for up to 3 months.

To Thaw and Serve
Thaw at cool room temperature. Reheat in a heavy-based saucepan, adding cheese toast and brandy as above.

ICED TOMATO AND BASIL SOUP

Make this colourful soup when tomatoes are plentiful and full of flavour

SERVES 4

450 g (1 lb) tomatoes, chopped

1 small onion, skinned and chopped

15 ml (1 tbsp) tomato purée

15 ml (1 tbsp) chopped fresh basil

600 ml (1 pint) chicken stock

salt and pepper

30 ml (2 tbsp) soured cream, to garnish (optional)

1 Purée the tomatoes, onion, tomato purée and basil in a blender or food processor. Pass through a sieve into a medium saucepan.

2 Stir in the stock. Heat gently to remove froth, then add salt and pepper to taste.

3 Chill before serving, garnished with swirls of soured cream, if liked.

To Freeze
Cool at the end of step 2, then pack without seasoning into rigid containers, leaving headspace. Freeze for up to 6 months.

To Thaw and Serve
Thaw overnight in the refrigerator. Add soured cream and adjust the seasoning before serving.

GOLDEN VEGETABLE SOUP

Add the turmeric sparingly to avoid overwhelming the fresh vegetable flavours

SERVES 4

25 g (1 oz) butter

1 large carrot, peeled and cut into 4 cm (1½ inch) matchsticks

2 celery sticks, cut into 4 cm (1½ inch) matchsticks

100 g (4 oz) swede, peeled and cut into 4 cm (1½ inch) matchsticks

225 g (8 oz) cauliflower, broken into florets

1 medium onion, skinned and sliced

2.5 ml (½ tsp) ground turmeric

1 litre (1¾ pints) vegetable stock

salt and pepper

snipped chives, to garnish

1 Melt the butter in a saucepan, add all the vegetables and cook for 2 minutes, stirring occasionally.
2 Add the turmeric and cook for 1 minute. Pour over the stock and adjust seasoning. Bring to the boil and simmer for 20 minutes. Garnish with snipped chives and serve with crusty brown bread.

To Freeze

Cool, then pack into rigid containers without the garnish, leaving headspace. Freeze for up to 3 months.

To Thaw and Serve

Thaw overnight in the refrigerator. Reheat in a heavy-based saucepan. Serve garnished with chives.

CHILLED PEA AND MINT SOUP

Freeze the sweet taste of fresh peas – and enjoy a taste of summer on winter days

SERVES 6

50 g (2 oz) butter

1 onion, skinned and roughly chopped

568 ml (1 pint) milk

600 ml (1 pint) chicken stock

900 g (2 lb) fresh peas, shelled

2 large mint sprigs

pinch of caster sugar

salt and pepper

150 ml (¼ pint) single cream

mint sprigs, to garnish

1 Melt the butter in a saucepan, add the onion, cover and cook gently for about 15 minutes until soft but not brown.
2 Remove from the heat and stir in the milk, stock, peas, the 2 mint sprigs, sugar and salt and pepper to taste. Bring to the boil, stirring.
3 Cover and simmer gently for about 30 minutes until the peas are very tender. Cool slightly, reserving about 45 ml (3 tbsp) peas for garnish. Rub the remaining peas through a sieve or purée in a blender or food processor until smooth.
4 Pour into a large bowl. Adjust seasoning, then cool. Stir in the cream and chill for 2–3 hours before serving. To serve, garnish with the reserved cooked peas and mint sprigs.

To Freeze

Cool at the end of step 3, then pack into rigid containers, leaving headspace. Freeze for up to 6 months.

To Thaw and Serve

Thaw overnight in the refrigerator. Adjust seasoning and whisk in the cream, then chill until ready to serve.

CREAM OF CARROT WITH ORANGE SOUP

A simple family soup with a sharp, fruity tang

SERVES 4–6

25 g (1 oz) butter
700 g (1½ lb) carrots, peeled and sliced
225 g (8 oz) onion, skinned and sliced
1 litre (1¾ pints) chicken or ham stock
1 orange
salt and pepper

1 Melt the butter in a saucepan, add the vegetables and cook gently for 10 minutes until softened slightly.
2 Add the stock and bring to the boil. Lower the heat, cover and simmer for about 40 minutes or until the vegetables are tender.
3 Sieve or purée the vegetables with half of the stock in a blender or food processor. Add this mixture to the stock remaining in the pan.
4 Meanwhile, pare half of the orange rind thinly, using a potato peeler, then cut it into shreds. Cook the shreds in gently boiling water until tender.
5 Finely grate the remaining orange rind into the soup. Stir well to combine.
6 Squeeze the juice of the orange into the pan. Reheat the soup gently, then taste and adjust seasoning. Drain the shreds of orange rind and use to garnish the soup just before serving.
Serve hot.

To Freeze
Cool, then pack into rigid containers, leaving headspace. Freeze for up to 3 months.

To Thaw and Serve
Reheat from frozen in a heavy-based saucepan.

SMOKED FISH CHOWDER

Serve this hearty main meal soup with crusty French bread

SERVES 4

1 large onion, skinned and grated
225 g (8 oz) potato, peeled and grated
100 g (4 oz) celery, finely chopped
450 g (1 lb) smoked haddock fillet, skinned
568 ml (1 pint) milk
salt and pepper
15 ml (1 tbsp) lemon juice
paprika, to garnish

1 Place the onion, potato, celery and 600 ml (1 pint) water into a saucepan, then bring to the boil. Lower the heat, cover and simmer for 10 minutes.
2 Add the fish and milk and bring back to the boil. Lower the heat, add salt and pepper to taste, then cover and simmer for 15 minutes until the fish is tender.
3 Using a slotted spoon, lift the fish out of the pan. Discard the fish bones and flake the flesh.
4 Return the flaked fish to the pan. Add the lemon juice, adjust seasoning and heat through gently. Serve hot, sprinkled with paprika.

To Freeze
Cool quickly, then pack into rigid containers without the lemon juice, leaving headspace. Freeze for up to 3 months.

To Thaw and Serve
Thaw overnight in the refrigerator. Reheat with the lemon juice in a heavy-based saucepan until heated through.

STARTERS AND SNACKS

CHICKEN LIVER PATE

Serve this rich creamy pâté with toast or as part of a lunch platter

SERVES 8

100 g (4 oz) butter
1 medium onion, skinned and chopped
1 garlic clove, skinned and crushed
450 g (1 lb) chicken livers, cleaned and dried
75 ml (5 tbsp) double cream
15 ml (1 tbsp) tomato purée
15 ml (1 tbsp) brandy
salt and pepper
pink peppercorns and bay leaves, to garnish

1 Melt 50 g (2 oz) of the butter in a saucepan, add the onion and garlic and fry gently for 5 minutes. Add the chicken livers and cook for 5 minutes.
2 Cool slightly, then add the cream, tomato purée, brandy and plenty of salt and pepper.
3 Purée the mixture in a blender or food processor. Spoon the pâté into a serving dish.
4 Melt the remaining butter gently. Pour the butter over the pâté and leave to cool. Chill for at least 2 hours. Garnish with peppercorns and bay leaves.

To Freeze
Spoon the pâté into a freezerproof dish, cover with melted butter and cool completely. Cover and freeze for up to 3 months.

To Thaw and Serve
Thaw overnight in the refrigerator. Garnish with peppercorns and bay leaves before serving.

COUNTRY MUSHROOMS

Mushrooms in a tarragon flavoured cream sauce make a refreshing first course

SERVES 4

25 g (1 oz) butter
450 g (1 lb) button mushrooms
15 ml (1 tbsp) plain flour
150 ml (¼ pint) milk
10 ml (2 tsp) wholegrain mustard
10 ml (2 tsp) chopped fresh tarragon or 2.5 ml (½ tsp) dried
45 ml (3 tbsp) soured cream
chicory and lettuce, to serve
tarragon leaves, to garnish

1 Melt the butter in a medium saucepan, add the mushrooms and fry for 2 minutes.
2 Stir in the flour and milk. Heat, stirring continuously until the sauce thickens, boils and is smooth. Simmer for 1–2 minutes.
3 Stir in the mustard, tarragon and soured cream.
4 Serve hot on a bed of chicory and lettuce leaves, garnished with tarragon.

To Freeze
Cool at the end of step 3, then pack into a rigid container, without garnish. Cover and freeze for up to 2 months.

To Thaw and Serve
Thaw, covered, at cool room temperature. Heat gently in a heavy-based saucepan and serve as above.

CRISPY CHICKEN PARCELS
Serve as a substantial meal starter or as a light snack

SERVES 4

25 g (1 oz) butter
50 g (2 oz) plain flour
300 ml (½ pint) milk
225 g (8 oz) cooked chicken, diced
15 ml (1 tbsp) chopped fresh tarragon or 10 ml (2 tsp) dried
75 g (3 oz) Gruyère cheese, grated
good pinch of ground mace
salt and pepper
15 ml (1 tbsp) vegetable oil
8–12 cannelloni tubes
180 ml (12 tbsp) dried breadcrumbs
180 ml (12 tbsp) grated Parmesan cheese
1 egg, beaten
oil, for deep-frying

1 Melt the butter in a heavy-based saucepan, add the flour and cook for 2 minutes, stirring. Remove from the heat and gradually stir in the milk. Bring to the boil, stirring constantly, then simmer for 3 minutes until thick and smooth.
2 Add the chicken, tarragon, Gruyère, mace and salt and pepper to taste, combining well.
3 Bring a large pan of salted water to the boil, then swirl in the oil. Drop in the cannelloni. Simmer for 5 minutes, drain.
4 Using a teaspoon, or a piping bag fitted with a large plain nozzle, fill each cannelloni tube with the chicken mixture. Pinch the edges to seal.
5 Mix the breadcrumbs and Parmesan in a shallow bowl. Dip the cannelloni tubes first in the beaten egg, then in the breadcrumbs and Parmesan, making sure they are evenly coated. Chill for 30 minutes.
6 Heat the oil in a deep-fat fryer to 180°C (350°F). Deep-fry the parcels, a few at a time, until golden brown and crisp. Drain on absorbent kitchen paper while frying the remainder. Serve hot.

To Freeze
Cool and pack into a rigid container, interleaved with greaseproof paper, at the end of step 5. Freeze for up to 3 months.

To Thaw and Serve
Thaw overnight in the refrigerator, then continue as step 6.

SMOKED TROUT PATE
Serve this rich fish pâté as a meal starter or as a light supper dish

SERVES 4

2 smoked trout, each weighing about 275 g (10 oz), skinned and boned
50 g (2 oz) butter, softened
30 ml (2 tbsp) lemon juice
60 ml (4 tbsp) single cream
pepper
pinch of ground mace
cucumber and lemon slices, to garnish

1 Put the trout flesh in a blender or food processor. Add the butter, lemon juice, cream, pepper and mace and blend together until smooth.
2 Divide the pâté equally between 4 ramekin dishes. Chill for 1 hour before serving. Garnish with cucumber and lemon slices. Serve accompanied with fingers of wholemeal toast.

To Freeze
Cover the ramekins with foil and overwrap in polythene bags. Freeze for up to 2 months.

To Thaw and Serve
Thaw, covered, overnight in the refrigerator. Garnish and serve.

QUICK PAN PIZZA

SERVES 4

75 g (3 oz) plain flour
salt and pepper
50 g (2 oz) butter
75 ml (3 fl oz) milk
100 g (4 oz) streaky bacon rashers, chopped
1 medium onion, skinned and sliced
4 tomatoes, skinned and chopped
30 ml (2 tbsp) tomato chutney
15 ml (1 tbsp) chopped fresh oregano
100 g (4 oz) mozzarella cheese, grated
fresh parsley and sliced tomato, to garnish

1 Put the flour and a pinch of salt into a bowl. Rub in 40 g (1¹/₂ oz) of the butter until the mixture resembles fine breadcrumbs. Add enough milk to form a soft dough. Roll out on a floured work surface to an 20.5 cm (8 inch) round.
2 Melt the remaining butter in a 20.5 cm (8 inch) frying pan and fry the dough on one side for 8 minutes until golden brown. Turn over.
3 Meanwhile, fry the bacon in its own fat with the onion until soft. Add the tomatoes, chutney and oregano. Add salt and pepper, then simmer gently for a few minutes.
4 Spread the tomato mixture over the pizza, then sprinkle with the mozzarella.
5 Cook gently for about 10 minutes. Brown under a hot grill, if preferred. Garnish with parsley and tomato.

To Freeze
Open freeze until solid, then wrap in foil. Freeze for up to 4 months.

To Thaw and Serve
Thaw overnight in the refrigerator. Reheat, wrapped in foil, in the oven at 180°C (350°F) mark 4 for 15 minutes, remove the foil and cook for 5 minutes to crisp.

MEXICAN BEEF TACOS

SERVES 4

30 ml (2 tbsp) vegetable oil
1 onion, skinned and finely chopped
1–2 garlic cloves, skinned and crushed
5–10 ml (1–2 tsp) chilli powder, or to taste
350 g (12 oz) lean minced beef
225 g (8 oz) can tomatoes
15 ml (1 tbsp) tomato purée
2.5 ml (¹/₂ tsp) sugar
salt and pepper
283 g (10 oz) can red kidney beans, rinsed
8 taco shells
shredded lettuce and grated cheese

1 Heat the oil in a pan, add the onion, garlic and chilli powder and fry gently until soft. Add the minced beef and fry until browned, stirring and pressing with a wooden spoon to remove any lumps.
2 Stir in the tomatoes with their juice and the tomato purée. Crush the tomatoes well with the spoon, then bring to the boil, stirring. Lower the heat, add the sugar and salt and pepper to taste. Simmer, uncovered, for 20 minutes until thick and reduced. Stir occasionally during this time to combine the ingredients and prevent sticking.
3 Add the kidney beans to the pan and heat through for 5 minutes. Meanwhile, heat the taco shells in the oven according to the instructions on the packet.
4 To serve, divide the mixture between the taco shells, then top with cheese and lettuce. Eat immediately.

To Freeze
Cool the meat mixture at the end of step 2, then pack into rigid containers, leaving headspace. Freeze for up to 3 months.

To Thaw and Serve
Thaw overnight in the refrigerator. Turn into a heavy pan and continue as above.

TURKEY TERRINE

SERVES 6–8

225 g (8 oz) cooked turkey meat
225 g (8 oz) turkey or pig's liver
175 g (6 oz) streaky bacon rashers
1 medium onion, skinned
225 g (8 oz) sausagemeat
1 garlic clove, skinned and crushed
15 ml (1 tbsp) chopped fresh sage
45 ml (3 tbsp) double cream
30 ml (2 tbsp) brandy
1 egg
salt and pepper
1 bay leaf

1 Mince the turkey, liver, 50 g (2 oz) of the bacon and the onion. Alternatively, work the ingredients in a food processor.
2 Put the minced mixture in a bowl. Add the sausagemeat, garlic, sage, cream, brandy, egg and salt and pepper to taste. Mix with a spoon to combine.
3 Stretch the remaining bacon rashers with a cook's knife.
4 Use the bacon rashers to completely line a 1.1 litre (2 pint) terrine or loaf tin.
5 Spoon the meat mixture into the container and place a bay leaf on top. Cover tightly with foil or a lid, then stand the container in a roasting tin.
6 Pour 4 cm (1½ inches) hot water into the roasting tin, then bake in the oven at 170°C (325°F) mark 3 for about 1½ hours. Remove from the water bath and leave to cool for 2 hours. Place heavy weights on top and chill overnight.
7 Turn out and cut into slices.

To Freeze
Unmould after step 6. Wrap in foil, then overwrap. Freeze for up to 2 months.

To Thaw and Serve
Thaw, unwrapped, in the refrigerator overnight. Serve cut into slices.

SPINACH PANCAKES

SERVES 6

75 g (3 oz) plain flour
pinch of salt
1 egg, size 6
450 ml (¾ pint) milk
50 g (2 oz) spinach, trimmed, washed and finely chopped
25 g (1 oz) butter, plus extra for frying
grated rind of ½ lemon
1 bay leaf
100 g (4 oz) smoked haddock, skinned and cubed
100 g (4 oz) cod, skinned and cubed

1 Sift 50 g (2 oz) of the flour and salt into a bowl. Break in the egg. Gradually add 150 ml (¼ pint) of the milk, beating to form a smooth batter. Stir in the spinach.
2 Heat a little butter in a 20.5 cm (8 inch) frying pan. When hot, pour in 45 ml (3 tbsp) batter, tilting the pan to cover the base. Cook until the pancake moves freely, turn, then cook until golden. Make 6 pancakes.
3 Put the remaining butter, flour and milk in a saucepan. Heat, whisking continuously, until the sauce thickens, boils and is smooth. Stir in the lemon rind, bay leaf and fish. Cook for 6 minutes.
4 Divide the mixture equally between the pancakes, then roll up. Serve hot.

To Freeze
Arrange the filled pancakes in foil containers and cool. Cover and freeze for up to 2 months.

To Thaw and Serve
To reheat from frozen, place containers on a baking sheet and loosen lids. Bake in the oven at 200°C (400°F) mark 6 for 30–40 minutes, removing lids for the last 5 minutes.

Feta Cheese Puffs with Basil

For the fullest flavour, look for feta cheese packed in brine or sold loose at the delicatessen

---

Makes 8

225 g (8 oz) feta cheese, grated
150 g (5 oz) natural yogurt
30 ml (2 tbsp) chopped fresh basil or 5 ml (1 tsp) dried
pepper
397 g (14 oz) packet frozen puff pastry, thawed
beaten egg, to glaze
basil leaves, to garnish

---

1 Mix the cheese with the yogurt, basil and pepper in a bowl. (Do not add salt as the cheese adds sufficient.)
2 Roll out the pastry thinly and cut out sixteen 10 cm (4 inch) rounds. Fold and reroll the pastry as necessary.
3 Place half the rounds on 2 baking sheets. Spoon the cheese mixture into the centre of each one.
4 Brush the pastry edges with egg. Cover with the remaining rounds, knocking up and pressing the pastry edges together to seal. Make a small slit in the top of each pastry puff.
5 Brush with beaten egg. Bake in the oven at 220°C (425°F) mark 7 for about 15 minutes or until well browned and crisp. Serve warm, garnished with basil leaves.

To Freeze
Open freeze the pastries on baking sheets, then wrap in foil. Freeze for up to 1 month.

To Thaw and Serve
Bake the frozen pastries in the oven at 220°C (425°F) mark 7 for about 25–35 minutes until browned and crisp.

Kebabs with Cumin

Serve on skewers for supper or in pockets of warm pitta bread as a handy snack

---

Serves 4

350 g (12 oz) finely minced veal or beef
finely grated rind of 1 small lemon
15 ml (1 tbsp) lemon juice
1 garlic clove, skinned and crushed
5 ml (1 tsp) ground cumin
2.5 ml (½ tsp) salt
2.5 ml (½ tsp) pepper
1 small onion, skinned and grated
vegetable oil, for grilling
lemon wedges, to serve

---

1 Put the minced meat in a bowl with the lemon rind and juice, the garlic, cumin and salt and pepper. Mix well together, preferably by hand.
2 Add the onion and mix again. (The longer the mixture is stirred, the drier it becomes and the easier it is to handle.) Cover the bowl and chill, preferably overnight.
3 Divide the mixture into 12 pieces and form into small sausage shapes. Chill again if possible.
4 Thread on to 4 oiled kebab skewers. Brush with oil and grill evenly for 10–12 minutes, turning frequently until browned. Serve hot, with lemon wedges.

To Freeze
Freeze at the end of step 3 in rigid containers, interleaving with greaseproof paper. Freeze for up to 3 months.

To Thaw and Serve
Thaw overnight in the refrigerator. Brush with a little oil, thead onto skewers and reheat under the grill.

ARABIC AUBERGINE DIP

SERVES 4–6

2 large aubergines, sliced

salt

2–3 garlic cloves, skinned and roughly chopped

10 ml (2 tsp) cumin seeds

100 ml (4 fl oz) olive oil

150 ml (¼ pint) tahini paste

about 100 ml (4 fl oz) lemon juice

thin tomato slices, to garnish

1 Place the aubergine slices in a colander and sprinkle each layer with salt. Cover with a plate, put heavy weights on top and leave for 30 minutes.

2 Meanwhile, crush the garlic and cumin seeds with a pestle and mortar. Add 5 ml (1 tsp) salt and mix well.

3 Rinse the aubergines under cold running water, then pat dry with absorbent kitchen paper. Heat the oil in a large, heavy-based frying pan until very hot. Add the aubergine slices in batches and fry until golden on both sides, turning once. Remove from the pan with a slotted spoon and drain again on paper.

4 Put the aubergine slices in a blender or food processor with the garlic mixture, tahini paste and about two-thirds of the lemon juice. Work to a smooth purée, then taste and add more lemon juice and salt if liked.

5 Turn the dip into a serving bowl, cover and chill until serving time. Serve chilled, garnished with tomato slices.

To Freeze

Pack into a rigid container without garnish, leaving headspace. Freeze for up to 3 months.

To Thaw and Serve

Thaw in the container overnight in the refrigerator. Stir well before serving.

OXFORD SAUSAGES

MAKES ABOUT 18

450 g (1 lb) lean boneless pork

450 g (1 lb) lean boneless veal

350 g (12 oz) shredded suet

225 g (8 oz) fresh breadcrumbs

grated rind of ½ lemon

5 ml (1 tsp) freshly grated nutmeg

15 ml (1 tbsp) chopped fresh mixed herbs or 5 ml (1 tsp) dried mixed herbs

5 ml (1 tsp) chopped fresh sage or a pinch of dried

salt and pepper

1 egg, lightly beaten

plain flour for coating

1 Mince or very finely chop the pork and veal. Put the minced meat in a large mixing bowl and add the suet, breadcrumbs, lemon rind, nutmeg and herbs. Mix together and season to taste. Add the egg to the mixture and mix well with a fork until all the ingredients are thoroughly combined and bound together.

2 With floured hands, form the mixture into sausage shapes. Coat each sausage in flour, shaking off any excess.

3 Cook the sausages under a hot grill, turning frequently, until evenly browned and cooked through. Serve the sausages with mashed potatoes and a green vegetable.

To Freeze

Freeze the sausages on a baking sheet at the end of step 2, then pack into rigid containers, interleaving with greaseproof paper. Freeze for up to 3 months.

To Thaw and Serve

Thaw in the refrigerator overnight. Complete step 3.

MEAT MAIN MEALS

BEEF HARE

This dish gets it's name from the spicy gamey flavour

SERVES 4

plain flour, to coat

salt and pepper

freshly grated nutmeg

900 g (2 lb) chuck steak, cut into 7.5 × 2.5 cm (3 × 1 inch) strips

5 ml (1 tsp) celery seeds

8 cloves

1 medium onion, skinned and quartered

1 small young parsnip, peeled and grated

150 ml (¼ pint) dry red wine

1 Season the flour with salt and pepper and plenty of nutmeg. Toss the meat in the seasoned flour to coat, shaking off any excess.
2 Place the meat in a deep 900 ml (1½ pint) casserole, scattering celery seeds in between the layers.
3 Stick 2 cloves into each onion quarter, then arrange the onion and parsnip on top of the meat. Pour in the wine, cover tightly and leave for about 2 hours.
4 Place in the oven at 220°C (425°F) mark 7 and immediately reduce the temperature to 170°C (325°F) mark 3. Cook for 2¼ hours or until the beef is tender.

To Freeze
Cool, then pack into rigid containers. Freeze for up to 3 months.

To Thaw and Serve
Thaw overnight in the refrigerator. Reheat in a tightly covered dish in the oven at 170°C (325°F) mark 3 for about 30 minutes.

DORSET JUGGED STEAK

SERVES 4

700 g (1½ lb) stewing steak, trimmed and cut into 2.5 cm (1 inch) cubes

25 g (1 oz) plain wholemeal flour

1 medium onion, skinned and sliced

4 cloves

salt and pepper

150 ml (¼ pint) port

about 450 ml (¾ pint) beef stock

225 g (8 oz) sausagemeat

50 g (2 oz) fresh wholemeal breadcrumbs

30 ml (2 tbsp) chopped fresh parsley

15 ml (1 tbsp) redcurrant jelly

1 Toss the meat in the flour, shaking off the excess, and put into casserole.
2 Add the onion and cloves and add salt and pepper to taste. Pour in the port and just enough stock to cover the meat.
3 Cover and cook in the oven at 170°C (325°F) mark 3 for about 3 hours until the meat is tender.
4 Meanwhile, mix together the sausagemeat, breadcrumbs and parsley and salt and pepper to taste. With floured hands, form the mixture into 8 balls.
5 Forty minutes before the end of the cooking time, stir the redcurrant jelly into the casserole. Add the forcemeat balls and cook, uncovered, until the forcemeat balls are cooked and slightly brown. Skim off any excess fat and serve hot.

To Freeze
Cook for 20 minutes after the forcemeat balls are added. Cool, then pack into rigid containers. Freeze for up to 3 months.

To Thaw and Serve
Thaw overnight in the refrigerator. Cook in the oven at 170°C (325°F) mark 3 for 30 minutes.

ITALIAN-STYLE MEATBALLS

SERVES 4

30 ml (2 tbsp) olive oil
1 large onion, skinned and finely chopped
2 garlic cloves, skinned and crushed
397 g (14 oz) can chopped tomatoes
10 ml (2 tsp) dried mixed herbs
10 ml (2 tsp) dried oregano
salt and pepper
450 g (1 lb) lean minced beef
50 g (2 oz) fresh white breadcrumbs
50 g (2 oz) Parmesan cheese, freshly grated
1 egg, beaten
20 small black olives, stoned
vegetable oil, for deep frying
100 ml (4 fl oz) dry red or white wine

1 Heat the oil in a heavy-based saucepan, add the onion and half of the crushed garlic and fry gently for about 5 minutes until soft and lightly coloured.
2 Add the tomatoes, half of the herbs and salt and pepper. Bring to the boil, stirring, cover and simmer for 20 minutes.
3 Meanwhile, make the meatballs. Put the minced beef in a bowl with the breadcrumbs, Parmesan, remaining garlic and herbs. Mix well with your hands, then add salt and pepper and bind with egg.
4 Pick up a small amount of the mixture about the size of a walnut. Press an olive in the centre, then shape the mixture around it. Make 20 meatballs.
5 Heat the oil in a deep-fryer to 190°C (375°F). Deep-fry the meatballs in batches for 2–3 minutes until lightly browned, then drain thoroughly.
6 Stir the wine into the tomato sauce, then add 300 ml (½ pint) water and the meatballs. Shake the pan to coat the meatballs in the sauce, adding more water if necessary. Cover and simmer for 15 minutes, adjust seasoning.

To Freeze
At the end of step 5, arrange the

meatballs in a rigid container. Add the wine to the sauce and spoon over. Freeze for up to 3 months.

To Thaw and Serve
Thaw overnight in the refrigerator. Reheat in a heavy-based saucepan.

BEEF WITH STOUT

SERVES 4

30 ml (2 tbsp) vegetable oil
700 g (1½ lb) stewing beef, trimmed and cut into 4 cm (1½ inch) cubes
2 large onions, skinned and sliced
15 ml (1 tbsp) plain flour
275 ml (9.68 fl oz) can stout
200 ml (7 fl oz) beef stock
30 ml (2 tbsp) tomato purée
100 g (4 oz) stoned prunes
225 g (8 oz) carrots, peeled and sliced
salt and pepper
croûtons, to garnish

1 Heat the oil in a flameproof casserole, add the meat and fry until well browned on all sides. Remove with a slotted spoon.
2 Add the onions to the remaining oil in the pan and fry gently until lightly browned. Stir in the flour and cook for 1 minute. Stir in the stout, stock, tomato purée, prunes and carrots. Bring to the boil and add salt and pepper to taste.
3 Replace the meat. Cover and cook in the oven at 170°C (325°F) mark 3 for 1½ –2 hours until tender. Add croûtons.

To Freeze
Cool, then pack without the croûtons. Freeze for up to 3 months.

To Thaw and Serve
Thaw overnight in the refrigerator. Reheat in a heavy-based saucepan and serve with croûtons.

LAMB KORMA

SERVES 4
2 onions, skinned and chopped
2.5 cm (1 inch) fresh root ginger, peeled
40 g (1½ oz) blanched almonds
2 garlic cloves, skinned
5 ml (1 tsp) ground cardamom
5 ml (1 tsp) ground cloves
5 ml (1 tsp) ground cinnamon
5 ml (1 tsp) ground cumin
5 ml (1 tsp) ground coriander
1.25 ml (¼ tsp) cayenne pepper
45 ml (3 tbsp) vegetable oil or ghee
900 g (2 lb) boned tender lamb, cubed
300 ml (½ pint) natural yogurt
salt and pepper
cucumber and lime slices, to garnish

1 Put the onions, ginger, almonds and
garlic in a blender or food processor with
90 ml (6 tbsp) water and blend to a
smooth paste. Add the spices and mix.
2 Heat the oil or ghee in a heavy-based
saucepan, add the lamb and fry for 5
minutes until browned on all sides.
3 Add the paste mixture and fry for
about 10 minutes, stirring, until the
mixture is lightly browned. Stir in the
yogurt gradually, add salt and pepper.
4 Cover with a tight-fitting lid and
simmer for 1¼–1½ hours until the meat
is really tender.
5 Transfer to a warmed serving dish and
serve garnished with cucumber and lime.

To Freeze
Cool at the end of step 4, then pack into
rigid containers. Freeze for up to 3
months.

To Thaw and Serve
Thaw overnight in the refrigerator. Reheat
in a tightly covered, heavy-based
saucepan over moderate heat.

BACON CHOPS WITH CIDER SAUCE

Choose thick, fresh bacon chops for this
tangy braise

SERVES 4
*4 bacon chops, each weighing about 175 g
(6 oz)*
15 ml (1 tbsp) prepared English mustard
25 g (1 oz) demerara sugar
300 ml (½ pint) dry cider
15 g (½ oz) butter
25 ml (1½ tbsp) plain flour
salt and pepper
chopped fresh parsley, to garnish

1 Put the chops side by side in a large
ovenproof dish. Mix the mustard and
sugar with enough cider to make a
smooth paste. Spread over the chops.
Leave for 30 minutes.
2 Cook in the oven at 200°C (400°F)
mark 6 for 15 minutes.
3 Meanwhile, put the butter, flour and
remaining cider in a saucepan. Heat,
whisking continuously, until the sauce
thickens, boils and is smooth. Simmer for
1–2 minutes. Add salt and pepper to taste.
4 Pour the sauce over the chops. Bake
for a further 15 minutes until cooked
through. Serve garnished with parsley.

To Freeze
Cool the sauce at the end of step 3, spoon
over the chops and cover. Freeze for up
to 1 month.

To Thaw and Serve
Thaw at cool room temperature. Cook in
the oven at 200°C (400°F) mark 6 for 25
minutes.

Right: Lamb Korma (page 64)
*Overleaf: Bath Buns (page 89), Cherry
and Coconut Cake (page 94) and Brown
Sugar Wheatmeals (page 92)*

BRAISED KIDNEYS IN PORT

SERVES 3
8 lambs' kidneys
25 g (1 oz) butter
1 medium onion, skinned and sliced
100 g (4 oz) mushrooms, sliced
45 ml (3 tbsp) plain flour
150 ml (¼ pint) port
150 ml (¼ pint) chicken stock
15 ml (1 tbsp) chopped fresh parsley
1 bouquet garni
salt and pepper

1 Skin the kidneys, then cut each one in half lengthways. Snip out the cores.
2 Heat the butter in a large frying pan or flameproof casserole, add the onion and fry for 3–4 minutes until softened. Add mushrooms and fry for 3–4 minutes.
3 Stir in the kidneys and cook for 5 minutes, stirring occasionally.
4 Stir in the flour, then gradually pour in the port and stock. Slowly bring to the boil, stirring well. Stir in the parsley and bouquet garni. Add salt and pepper.
5 Cover and simmer for 15 minutes, stirring occasionally. Remove the bouquet garni and serve hot with boiled rice or mashed potatoes.

To Freeze
Cool, discard the bouquet garni, then pack into a rigid container. Freeze for up to 3 months.

To Thaw and Serve
Thaw overnight in the refrigerator. Turn into a heavy-based saucepan and reheat gently.

Left: Haddock and Mushroom Puffs and Spanish Cod (page 74)
Previous page: Leek and Pea Flan (page 77) and Spicy Chick-Peas and Swede (page 78)

LAMB AND PEPPER KEBABS

SERVES 4–6
700 g (1½ lb) lamb fillet, trimmed
100 ml (4 fl oz) dry white wine
100 ml (4 fl oz) corn oil
50 ml (2 fl oz) lemon juice
2 celery sticks, very finely chopped
1 small onion, skinned and grated
2 garlic cloves, skinned and crushed
1 large tomato, skinned and finely chopped
20 ml (4 tsp) chopped fresh thyme or 10 ml (2 tsp) dried
salt and pepper
1 medium red pepper
1 medium green pepper
few bay leaves

1 Cut the lamb into cubes and place in a bowl. In a jug, whisk together the wine, oil, lemon juice, celery, onion, garlic, tomato, thyme and salt and pepper.
2 Pour the marinade over the lamb and turn the meat until well coated. Cover the bowl and marinate in the refrigerator for 4 hours, preferably overnight.
3 When ready to cook, cut the tops off the peppers and remove the cores and seeds. Cut the flesh into squares.
4 Thread the lamb, peppers and bay leaves on to oiled skewers. Coat with the marinade, reserving the remainder.
5 Cook over charcoal or under a preheated moderate grill for 20–25 minutes until the lamb is tender. Turn the skewers frequently during cooking and brush with the reserved marinade.

To Freeze
At the end of step 2, pack the lamb and marinade into rigid containers. Freeze for up to 3 months.

To Thaw and Serve
Thaw overnight in the refrigerator. Complete steps 3, 4 and 5.

LOIN OF LAMB WITH APRICOT AND HERB STUFFING

Use only previously unfrozen lamb for this fruity roast and ask the butcher to bone the joint for you

SERVES 6

15 g (½ oz) butter

1 medium onion, skinned and finely chopped

30 ml (2 tbsp) chopped fresh thyme or mint

75 g (3 oz) fresh wholemeal breadcrumbs

salt and pepper

100 g (4 oz) no-soak dried apricots, finely chopped

1 egg, beaten

1.6 kg (3½ lb) loin of lamb, boned

thyme or mint sprigs, to garnish

1 Melt the butter in a large frying pan, add the onion and fry for 5 minutes until softened. Stir in the thyme, breadcrumbs and salt and pepper. Set the stuffing aside to cool.
2 Add the apricots to the mixture with the egg and mix well together.
3 Lay the meat out flat, fat side down, then spread the apricot stuffing over the lamb.
4 Roll up the meat to enclose the stuffing and tie with strong cotton or fine string at regular intervals. Put the joint in a roasting tin.
5 Roast in the oven at 180°C (350°F) mark 4 for about 2 hours or until cooked to your liking. To serve, remove the string and carve into thick slices. Garnish with thyme or mint.

To Freeze
Pack into a rigid container after rolling and tying. Freeze for up to 3 months.

To Thaw and Serve
Thaw overnight in the refrigerator. Complete steps 4 and 5.

LIKKY PIE

SERVES 4

225 g (8 oz) leeks, trimmed, sliced and washed

salt and pepper

450 g (1 lb) lean boneless pork, cut into 2.5 cm (1 inch) cubes

150 ml (¼ pint) milk

75 ml (3 fl oz) single cream

2 eggs, lightly beaten

212 g (7½ oz) packet frozen puff pastry, thawed

1 Parboil the leeks in a saucepan of boiling salted water for about 5 minutes. Drain well. Place the leeks and pork in a 1.1 litre (2 pint) pie dish. Add salt and pepper to taste and pour in the milk.
2 Cover with foil and cook in the oven at 200°C (400°F) mark 6 for about 1 hour. (It does not matter if it looks curdled.)
3 Stir the cream into the eggs, then pour into the dish. Leave to cool.
4 Roll out the pastry on a lightly floured surface to 5 cm (2 inches) wider than the dish. Cut a 2.5 cm (1 inch) strip from the outer edge and use to line the dampened rim of the pie dish. Dampen the pastry rim with water, cover with the pastry lid and seal the edges well, then knock up and flute. Make a hole in the centre of the pie and use pastry trimmings to decorate.
5 Bake at 220°C (425°F) mark 7 for 25–30 minutes until risen and golden.

To Freeze
At step 4, complete the pie without piercing the top, then overwrap with foil. Freeze for up to 3 months.

To Thaw and Serve
Thaw overnight in the refrigerator. Unwrap and bake in the oven at 220°C (425°F) mark 7 for 25–35 minutes until well risen and golden brown.

PORK PAPRIKASH

SERVES 4

50 g (2 oz) butter
30 ml (2 tbsp) olive oil
900 g (2 lb) boneless pork sparerib, trimmed and cut into cubes
450 g (1 lb) Spanish onions, skinned and thinly sliced
2 garlic cloves, skinned and crushed (optional)
15 ml (1 tbsp) paprika
10 ml (2 tsp) caraway seeds
450 ml (³/₄ pint) chicken stock
salt and pepper
about 150 ml (¹/₄ pint) soured cream and snipped chives, to finish

1 Heat 25 g (1 oz) of the butter with the oil in a flameproof casserole, add the cubes of pork and fry over high heat for about 5 minutes until coloured on all sides. Remove with a slotted spoon.
2 Reduce the heat to very low and melt the remaining butter in the pan. Add the onions and garlic, if using, and fry very gently for about 30 minutes until very soft and golden, stirring frequently.
3 Stir the paprika and caraway seeds into the onions, then add the pork and juices and mix well. Pour in the stock, add salt and pepper to taste and bring slowly to the boil, stirring. Cover and cook gently for about 1¹/₂ hours until tender.
4 Before serving, taste and adjust seasoning. Drizzle over soured cream and sprinkle with chives. Serve hot.

To Freeze
Cool after step 3, then pack into rigid containers. Freeze for up to 3 months.

To Thaw and Serve
Thaw overnight in the refrigerator. Reheat in a heavy-based saucepan, then complete step 4.

CHINESE PORK AND GINGER CASSEROLE

SERVES 4

30 ml (2 tbsp) vegetable oil
1 small onion, skinned and finely chopped
2.5 cm (1 inch) piece fresh root ginger, peeled
700 g (1¹/₂ lb) boneless lean pork, such as shoulder or sparerib, cubed
30 ml (2 tbsp) dry sherry
15 ml (1 tbsp) soy sauce
300 ml (¹/₂ pint) dry or American ginger ale
2.5 ml (¹/₂ tsp) five-spice powder
salt and pepper
50 g (2 oz) stem ginger, sliced
¹/₂ red pepper, cored, seeded and sliced
¹/₂ yellow pepper, cored, seeded and sliced

1 Heat the oil in a flameproof casserole, add the onion and fry gently for 5 minutes until soft but not coloured.
2 Meanwhile, crush the root ginger with a mortar and pestle. Add the crushed ginger to the casserole with the pork, increase the heat and fry until the meat is browned on all sides.
3 Stir in the sherry and soy sauce, then the ginger ale, five-spice powder and salt and pepper to taste. Bring slowly to the boil, stirring, then lower the heat, cover and simmer for about 1 hour until the pork is just tender.
4 Add the stem ginger and pepper slices to the casserole and continue cooking for a further 10 minutes. Serve hot.

To Freeze
Cool at the end of step 3, then pack into rigid containers. Freeze for up to 3 months.

To Thaw and Serve
Thaw overnight in the refrigerator. Continue as above.

PORK FILLET IN WINE AND CORIANDER

SERVES 4

700 g (1½ lb) pork fillet or tenderloin, trimmed and cut into 1.25 cm (½ inch) slices
15 g (½ oz) butter
15 ml (1 tbsp) vegetable oil
1 small green pepper, seeded and sliced into rings
1 medium onion, skinned and chopped
15 g (½ oz) plain flour
15 ml (1 tbsp) coriander seeds, ground
150 ml (¼ pint) chicken stock
150 ml (¼ pint) dry white wine
salt and pepper

1 Place the pork between 2 sheets of greaseproof paper and flatten with a mallet or rolling pin until thin.
2 Melt the butter and oil in a large saucepan, add the pork and brown on both sides. Add the pepper and onion and lightly cook for 8–10 minutes until softened.
3 Stir in the flour and coriander and cook for 1 minute. Gradually add the stock and wine, stirring until the sauce thickens, boils and is smooth. Season to taste. Simmer gently for 5–10 minutes, until the pork is tender and cooked through.

To Freeze
Cool, then pack into rigid containers. Freeze for up to 3 months.

To Thaw and Serve
Thaw overnight in the refrigerator. Reheat in a heavy-based saucepan.

SAUSAGE AND BEAN STEW

SERVES 4

15 ml (1 tbsp) vegetable oil
15 g (½ oz) butter
450 g (1 lb) pork sausages
1 large onion, skinned and sliced
two 397 g (14 oz) cans red kidney beans, drained
227 g (8 oz) can tomatoes
30 ml (2 tbsp) tomato purée
350 ml (12 fl oz) dry cider
salt and pepper

1 Heat the oil and butter in a large flameproof casserole and fry the sausages for about 5 minutes until browned. Cut each sausage in half crossways.
2 Add the onions to the casserole and fry for 5 minutes until golden brown. Drain off any excess fat. Return the sausages to the casserole together with the beans, tomatoes and their juice, tomato purée, cider and salt and pepper to taste.
3 Cover and cook gently for about 15 minutes or until the sausages are tender. Accompany with crusty bread, boiled rice or mashed potatoes.

To Freeze
Cool, then pack into rigid containers. Freeze for up to 3 months.

To Thaw and Serve
Thaw overnight in the refrigerator. Reheat in a heavy-based saucepan.

POULTRY MAIN MEALS

SPICED CHICKEN

This simple chicken curry improves in flavour after freezing

SERVES 4

350 g (12 oz) boneless chicken, skinned and diced
40 g (1½ oz) plain wholemeal flour
5 ml (1 tsp) curry powder
2.5 ml (½ tsp) cayenne pepper
40 g (1½ oz) butter
1 medium onion, skinned and chopped
450 ml (¾ pint) milk
60 ml (4 tbsp) apple chutney
100 g (4 oz) sultanas
150 ml (¼ pint) soured cream
2.5 ml (½ tsp) paprika

1 Toss the chicken in the flour, curry powder and cayenne pepper, shaking off any excess.
2 Melt the butter in a large saucepan, add the chicken and onion and lightly fry for 5–6 minutes until the chicken is brown and the onion lightly coloured.
3 Stir in the remaining flour. Gradually blend in the milk, stirring until the sauce thickens, boils and is smooth.
4 Add the chutney and sultanas and simmer gently for 30–35 minutes until the chicken is tender.
5 Remove the pan from the heat and drizzle with the cream. Sprinkle with the paprika and serve with boiled rice.

To Freeze
Cool at the end of step 4, then pack. Freeze for up to 3 months.

To Thaw and Serve
Thaw overnight in the refrigerator. Reheat in a heavy-based saucepan over moderate heat. Complete step 5.

CHICKEN CROQUETTES

SERVES 2
50 g (2 oz) butter
60 ml (4 tbsp) plain flour
200 ml (⅓ pint) milk
grated rind of ½ lemon
15 ml (1 tbsp) capers, chopped
175 g (6 oz) cooked chicken, minced
15 ml (1 tbsp) chopped fresh parsley
salt and pepper
1 egg, beaten
50 g (2 oz) dry white breadcrumbs
vegetable oil, for frying
lemon wedges, to garnish

1 Melt the butter in a saucepan, add the flour and cook gently, stirring, for 2 minutes. Remove from the heat and gradually stir in the milk. Bring to the boil and simmer for about 3 minutes, stirring, until the sauce is smooth and thick.
2 Add the lemon rind, capers and chicken with the parsley and salt and pepper to taste. Mix well together. Cool for 30 minutes, then chill for 2–3 hours or preferably overnight.
3 Shape the mixture into 6 even-sized croquettes. Dip in the beaten egg, then roll in the breadcrumbs to coat.
4 Heat a deep-fat fryer to 180°C (350°F), then deep-fry or shallow fry in hot oil for about 10 minutes or until golden brown. Serve hot, with lemon wedges.

To Freeze
At step 3, pack the croquettes into rigid containers, interleaving with greaseproof paper. Freeze for up to 2 months.

To Thaw and Serve
Thaw, loosely covered, overnight in the refrigerator. Continue step 4.

CHICKEN IN RED WINE WITH RAISINS

Cooked in it's spicy fruit marinade, this chicken takes on a wonderful flavour

SERVES 4
300 ml (½ pint) red wine
45 ml (3 tbsp) red wine vinegar
100 g (4 oz) seedless raisins
175 g (6 oz) no-soak dried apricots, halved
5 ml (1 tsp) ground ginger
5 ml (1 tsp) ground cinnamon
1 cm (½ inch) piece fresh root ginger, peeled and grated
4 cloves
4 juniper berries, lightly crushed
4 chicken breast fillets, with skin on, each weighing about 175 g (6 oz)
30 ml (2 tbsp) plain wholemeal flour
salt and pepper
15 g (½ oz) butter
15 ml (1 tbsp) vegetable oil
300 ml (½ pint) chicken stock
orange segments, to garnish

1 Put the wine, vinegar, raisins, apricots, ground ginger, cinnamon, fresh ginger, cloves and juniper berries in a dish. Add the chicken breasts and spoon the liquid over them. Cover and leave to marinate in a cool place for 3–4 hours or overnight.

2 Remove the chicken from the marinade and dry with absorbent kitchen paper. Reserve the marinade. Season the flour with salt and pepper, then use to coat the chicken. Heat the butter and oil in a large flameproof casserole, add the chicken, skin side down, and fry until lightly browned, turn over and fry the other side. Drain on absorbent kitchen paper.

3 Pour off any excess fat from the casserole, then stir in the chicken stock, reserved marinade and fruit and bring to the boil. Return the chicken to the casserole, cover tightly and cook for about 30 minutes until the chicken is tender.

4 Transfer the chicken to a warmed serving dish and keep warm. Boil the liquid until reduced and thickened, then pour over the chicken. Serve garnished with orange segments. Accompany with boiled rice.

To Freeze
Cool at the end of step 3, then pack into rigid containers. Freeze for up to 3 months.

To Thaw and Serve
Thaw overnight in the refrigerator. Reheat the chicken in a heavy-based saucepan, then complete step 4.

CHICKEN AND BEAN LAYER

SERVES 4
40 g (1½ oz) butter
40 g (1½ oz) plain wholemeal flour
568 ml (1 pint) milk
75 g (3 oz) Red Leicester cheese, grated
2.5 ml (½ tsp) mustard powder
2.5 ml (½ tsp) cayenne pepper
freshly ground pepper
450 g (1 lb) green beans, cooked
450 g (1 lb) boned cooked chicken, skinned and chopped
50 g (2 oz) no-soak dried apricots, chopped
25 g (1 oz) flaked almonds

1 Put the butter, flour and milk in a saucepan. Heat, whisking continuously, until the sauce thickens, boils and is smooth. Simmer for 2–3 minutes. Remove the pan from the heat, add the cheese, mustard and peppers, then stir until the cheese has melted.
2 Layer the beans, chicken, apricots and sauce in a 1.7 litre (3 pint) ovenproof serving dish. Sprinkle with almonds.
3 Bake, uncovered, at 180°C (350°F) mark 4 for 25 minutes. Serve with baked potatoes.

To Freeze
Cool the sauce at the end of step 1. Pack the remaining ingredients into a freezeproof dish and pour over the sauce. Open freeze, then cover. Freeze for up to 2 months.

To Thaw and Serve
Cook from frozen in the oven at 180°C (350°F) mark 4 for about 50 minutes or until piping hot.

CHICKEN IN WHITE WINE

SERVES 6
100 g (4 oz) lean bacon, rinded and diced
450 g (1 lb) button onions, skinned
225 g (8 oz) button mushrooms
6 chicken quarters, halved
50 g (2 oz) plain flour
salt and pepper
25 g (1 oz) butter
30 ml (2 tbsp) vegetable oil
300 ml (½ pint) dry white wine
300 ml (½ pint) chicken stock
1 garlic clove, skinned and crushed
sprigs of fresh thyme or 2.5 ml (½ tsp) dried
2 bay leaves
chopped fresh parsley, to garnish

1 Fry the bacon in its own fat in a large frying pan until beginning to brown. Add the onions and fry until browned, then add the mushrooms and fry for 2 minutes. Transfer to a casserole.
2 Coat the chicken joints with the flour, seasoned with salt and pepper. Heat the butter and the oil in the frying pan, add the chicken and fry until browned all over. Transfer the chicken to the casserole.
3 Gradually stir the white wine into the frying pan. Bring to the boil, stirring, then pour over the chicken joints.
4 Add the chicken stock, garlic, herbs and seasoning to taste to the frying pan. Bring to the boil, then pour over the chicken.
5 Cover and cook in the oven at 170°C (325°F) mark 3 for 1 hour or until the chicken is tender. Skim any fat from the cooking liquid. Garnish.

To Freeze
Cool, then pack into rigid containers. Freeze for up to 3 months.

To Thaw and Serve
Thaw overnight in the refrigerator. Reheat in a covered dish at 170°C (325°F) mark 3 for about 30 minutes.

BAKED TURKEY ESCALOPES WITH CRANBERRY AND COCONUT

Serve this unusual main course dish with a green salad or vegetables in a creamy sauce

SERVES 4
450 g (1 lb) boneless turkey breast
salt and pepper
20 ml (4 tsp) Dijon mustard
60 ml (4 tbsp) cranberry sauce
15 g (½ oz) plain flour
1 egg, beaten
15 g (½ oz) desiccated coconut
40 g (1½ oz) fresh breadcrumbs
50 g (2 oz) butter

1 Thinly slice the turkey breast into 4. Bat out into escalopes between sheets of damp greaseproof paper or cling film. Add salt and pepper, then spread each portion with mustard and cranberry sauce.
2 Roll up, starting from the thin end, and secure with a wooden cocktail stick or toothpick. Dust each portion with flour, then brush with egg. Combine the coconut and breadcrumbs, then coat the turkey with the mixture.
3 Melt the butter in a frying pan, add the turkey portions and fry until brown on both sides. Transfer to a baking tin just large enough to take the turkey in a single layer and baste with more butter. Bake in the oven at 180°C (350°F) mark 4 for about 40 minutes until tender.

To Freeze
At the end of step 2, put the turkey escalopes into a rigid container, interleaving with greaseproof paper. Freeze for up to 1 month.

To Thaw and Serve
Thaw overnight in the refrigerator, then complete step 3.

TURKEY AND LEEK CRUMBLE

SERVES 4
75 g (3 oz) butter
450 g (1 lb) boneless turkey, skinned and cubed
150 g (5 oz) plain wholemeal flour
450 ml (¾ pint) milk
salt and pepper
10 ml (2 tsp) chopped fresh sage
450 g (1 lb) leeks, trimmed, sliced and washed
100 g (4 oz) small button mushrooms
5 ml (1 tsp) mustard powder
5 ml (1 tsp) paprika
50 g (2 oz) Cheddar cheese, grated
25 g (1 oz) porridge oats

1 Melt 25 g (1 oz) of the butter in a large saucepan, add the turkey and fry for 5–6 minutes until lightly browned.
2 Stir in 25 g (1 oz) of the flour and cook for 2–3 minutes, then gradually blend in the milk. Heat, whisking continuously, until the sauce thickens, boils and is smooth. Simmer gently for 15 minutes. Add salt and pepper to taste.
3 Add the sage, leeks and mushrooms to the sauce and simmer for 10 minutes.
4 Rub the remaining butter into the remaining flour, the mustard and paprika, then stir in the cheese and oats.
5 Pour the turkey and leek sauce into a 1.7 litre (3 pint) ovenproof serving dish. Sprinkle with the crumble mixture. Bake in the oven at 200°C (400°F) mark 6 for 25 minutes.

To Freeze
Open freeze after adding the crumble topping, then cover. Freeze for up to 3 months.

To Thaw and Serve
Thaw overnight in the refrigerator, then cook from frozen in the oven at 200°C (400°F) mark 6 for 25–35 minutes.

FISH MAIN MEALS

SEAFOOD CURRY

SERVES 4
45 ml (3 tbsp) vegetable oil
2 onions, skinned and sliced into rings
25 g (1 oz) desiccated coconut
15 ml (1 tbsp) plain flour
5 ml (1 tsp) ground coriander
450 g (1 lb) fresh haddock fillet, skinned and cut into chunks
1 fresh green chilli, halved, seeded and finely chopped
150 ml (¼ pint) white wine
25 g (1 oz) salted peanuts
100 g (4 oz) frozen prawns, thawed, drained and thoroughly dried
salt and pepper
coriander sprigs and shredded coconut, toasted, to garnish

1 Heat the oil in a large sauté pan, add the onion rings and cook until browned.
2 Mix the coconut, flour and coriander together and toss with the haddock and chilli. Add to the pan and fry gently for 5–10 minutes until golden, stirring.
3 Pour in the wine, bring to boil and add the peanuts, prawns and salt and pepper to taste. Cover tightly and simmer for 5–10 minutes or until the fish is tender. To serve, garnish with coriander and coconut.

To Freeze
Omit the peanuts, then complete step 3. Cool and pack in rigid containers. Freeze for up to 1 month.

To Thaw and Serve
Thaw overnight in the refrigerator. Turn into a heavy-based saucepan, add the peanuts and reheat gently.

TARRAGON STUFFED TROUT

SERVES 6
100 g (4 oz) peeled prawns
50 g (2 oz) butter
100 g (4 oz) onion, skinned and finely chopped
225 g (8 oz) button mushrooms, chopped
5 ml (1 tsp) chopped fresh tarragon or 1.25 ml (¼ tsp) dried
salt and pepper
25 g (1 oz) long-grain rice, cooked
30 ml (2 tbsp) lemon juice
6 trout, about 225 g (8 oz) each, cleaned
tarragon sprigs, to garnish

1 To make the stuffing, cut each of the peeled prawns into 2–3 pieces. Melt the butter in a large frying pan, add the onion and fry for 5 minutes until golden brown.
2 Add the mushrooms with the tarragon and salt and pepper and cook over high heat for 5–10 minutes until all excess moisture has evaporated. Cool.
3 Mix the prawns, rice, lemon juice and mushroom mixture together and add salt and pepper to taste.
4 Place the fish side by side in a lightly buttered ovenproof dish and spoon the stuffing into the fish. Cover and cook in the oven at 180°C (350°F) mark 4 for about 30 minutes. Garnish.

To Freeze
Complete step 3, then lay the trout on sheets of foil and spoon in the stuffing. Wrap in parcels, sealing completely. Freeze for up to 2 months.

To Thaw and Serve
Thaw overnight in the refrigerator. Continue as above.

HADDOCK AND MUSHROOM PUFFS

SERVES 4

397 g (14 oz) packet puff pastry, thawed
450 g (1 lb) haddock fillet, skinned
213 g (7½ oz) can creamed mushrooms
5 ml (1 tsp) lemon juice
20 ml (4 tsp) capers, chopped
15 ml (1 tbsp) snipped fresh chives
salt and pepper
1 egg, beaten, to glaze

1 Roll out the pastry on a floured surface into a 40.5 cm (16 inch) square. Using a sharp knife, cut into 4 squares, trim the edges and reserve the pastry trimmings.
2 Place the squares on dampened baking sheets. Divide the fish into 4 and place diagonally across the pastry.
3 Combine the creamed mushrooms with the lemon juice, capers, chives and salt and pepper to taste. Mix well, then spoon over the pieces of haddock.
4 Brush the edges of each square lightly with water. Bring the 4 points of each square together and seal the edges to form an envelope-shaped parcel.
5 Decorate with pastry trimmings and make a small hole in the centre of each parcel. Chill for 30 minutes.
6 Beat the egg with a pinch of salt and use to glaze the pastry. Bake in the oven at 220°C (425°F) mark 7 for about 20 minutes until golden and well risen.

To Freeze
Freeze the pastries on baking sheets at step 6, then pack into rigid containers, interleaving with greaseproof paper. Freeze for up to 1 month.

To Thaw and Serve
Bake the frozen pastries in the oven at 220°C (425°F) mark 7 for about 30 minutes until golden and well risen.

SPANISH COD WITH PEPPERS, TOMATOES AND GARLIC

SERVES 4

700 g (1½ lb) cod fillets
1 litre (1¾ pints) mussels
30 ml (2 tbsp) vegetable oil
2 onions, skinned and sliced
1 red pepper, cored, seeded and sliced
1 green pepper, cored, seeded and sliced
1–2 garlic cloves, skinned and crushed
450 g (1 lb) tomatoes, skinned and chopped
300 ml (½ pint) white wine
2.5 ml (½ tsp) Tabasco sauce
1 bay leaf
salt and pepper

1 Using a sharp knife, skin the cod and cut it into chunks.
2 Scrub the mussels, discarding any which are open. Place in a saucepan, cover and cook over a high heat for about 8 minutes or until the mussels have opened. Shell all but 4 mussels.
3 Heat the oil in a pan, add the onions, peppers and garlic and cook for about 5 minutes. Add the tomatoes and wine, simmer for 5 minutes, then add the Tabasco.
4 Layer the fish and vegetables in a casserole, then add the bay leaf and salt and pepper. Pour over the wine. Push the 4 mussels in shells into the top layer. Cover and cook in the oven at 180°C (350°F) mark 4 for 1 hour. Serve hot.

To Freeze
Bake in a freezerproof dish for 30 minutes, then cool and cover. Wrap whole mussels separately. Freeze for up to 1 month.

To Thaw and Serve
Thaw overnight with mussels in the refrigerator. Cook at 180°C (350°F) mark 4 for about 30 minutes.

SOMERSET FISH CASSEROLE

SERVES 4

900 g (2 lb) brill or coley fillets, skinned
50 g (2 oz) plain flour
salt and pepper
65 g (2½ oz) butter
1 medium onion, skinned and finely chopped
300 ml (½ pint) dry cider
10 ml (2 tsp) anchovy essence
15 ml (1 tbsp) lemon juice
1 eating apple
chopped fresh parsley, to garnish

1 Cut the fish into 5 cm (2 inch) chunks. Season 25 g (1 oz) of the flour with salt and pepper, then use to coat the fish.
2 Melt 25 g (1 oz) of the butter in a saucepan, add the onion and cook gently for 5 minutes. Add the fish and cook for 3 minutes or until lightly browned. Remove the fish and onion to a buttered ovenproof dish.
3 To make the sauce, add 25 g (1 oz) of the butter to that remaining the pan, then add the remaining flour and cook, stirring, for 1 minute. Gradually stir in the cider, anchovy essence and lemon juice. Simmer for 2–3 minutes until thick.
4 Pour the sauce over the fish. Cook at 180°C (350°F) mark 4 for 20 minutes.
5 Meanwhile, peel, core and slice the apple into rings, then fry the apple rings in the remaining butter for 1–2 minutes. Drain and top the fish. Garnish.

To Freeze
Cool the sauce at the end of step 3. Pack the fish and onion in a container and pour over sauce. Freeze for up to 2 months.

To Thaw and Serve
Thaw overnight in the refrigerator. Place in an ovenproof dish and bake in the oven at 180°C (350°F) mark 4 for 20–30 minutes. Serve with apple and parsley.

SMOKED HADDOCK BAKE

SERVES 4

450 g (1 lb) smoked haddock fillets, skinned
750 ml (1¼ pints) fresh milk
25 g (1 oz) butter
40 g (1½ oz) plain wholemeal flour
100 g (4 oz) Red Leicester cheese, grated
pepper
100 g (4 oz) oven-ready wholewheat lasagne

1 Put the haddock in a large saucepan with the milk. Bring to the simmering point, cover, then simmer for 10–15 minutes, until tender. Drain, reserving the milk, then flake the fish, discarding any bones. Set aside while making the sauce.
2 Put the butter, flour and reserved milk in a saucepan. Heat, whisking continuously, until the sauce thickens, boils and is smooth. Simmer for 1–2 minutes. Remove the pan from the heat and add 50 g (2 oz) of the Red Leicester, the haddock and pepper. Stir carefully to mix.
3 Layer the sauce and lasagne sheets in an ovenproof serving dish, starting and finishing with the sauce. Sprinkle the remaining cheese on top. Bake at 190°C (375°F) mark 5 for 30–35 minutes until golden brown.

To Freeze
Cool, open freeze, then cover. Freeze for up to 3 months.

To Thaw and Serve
Cook from frozen in the oven at 180°C (350°F) mark 4 for about 50–60 minutes or until piping hot.

STUFFED HERRINGS

SERVES 4

65 g (2½ oz) butter

1 medium onion, skinned and finely chopped

50 g (2 oz) fresh wholemeal breadcrumbs

50 g (2 oz) shelled walnut pieces, roughly chopped

15 ml (1 tbsp) prepared English mustard

finely grated rind and juice of 1 lemon

45 ml (3 tbsp) chopped fresh mixed herbs, such as chives, parsley, rosemary, thyme

salt and pepper

4 medium herrings, each weighing about 275 g (10 oz), cleaned, boned and heads and tails removed

1 Melt 15 g (½ oz) of the butter in a saucepan, add the onion and fry gently for about 5 minutes until softened, stirring occasionally.

2 Meanwhile, mix together the breadcrumbs, walnuts, mustard, lemon rind, 15 ml (1 tbsp) lemon juice and mixed herbs. Season to taste. Add the onion and mix together well.

3 Open the herring fillets and lay skin side down. Press the stuffing mixture evenly over each fillet. Fold the herring fillets back in half and slash the skin several times.

4 Melt the remaining butter in a large frying pan, add the fish and fry for about 10 minutes, turning them once, until they are tender and browned on each side.

To Freeze

Complete step 2, then lay the herrings on sheets of greaseproof paper and complete step 3. Wrap in parcels, sealing completely. Overwrap. Freeze for up to 2 months.

To Thaw and Serve

Thaw in the wrappings at cool room temperature. Complete step 4.

FISH CAKES WITH HERBS

SERVES 4

275 g (10 oz) haddock, skinned and boned

15 ml (1 tbsp) lemon juice

15 ml (1 tbsp) Worcestershire sauce

15 ml (1 tbsp) creamed horseradish

100 ml (4 fl oz) milk

15 ml (1 tbsp) snipped fresh chives

15 ml (1 tbsp) chopped fresh parsley

350 g (12 oz) potatoes, cooked and mashed

50 g (2 oz) fresh wholemeal breadcrumbs

1 Purée the fish in a blender or food processor with the lemon juice, Worcestershire sauce and horseradish. Stir in the milk, chives, parsley and potatoes.

2 Shape the mixture into 4 fish cakes and coat with breadcrumbs.

3 Grill under a moderate heat for 5 minutes on each side until browned. Serve with a tomato sauce and salad.

To Freeze

Freeze the fish cakes on a baking sheet at the end of step 2, then pack into rigid containers, interleaving with greaseproof paper. Freeze for up to 3 months.

To Thaw and Serve

Thaw in the refrigerator overnight. Complete step 3.

VEGETARIAN MAIN MEALS

LEEK AND PEA FLAN
Serve this pretty green flan for lunch or supper with salad

SERVES 4

450 g (1 lb) leeks, trimmed, sliced and washed

100 g (4 oz) fresh or frozen peas

salt and pepper

150 ml (¼ pint) milk

150 g (5 oz) natural yogurt

3 eggs

175 g (6 oz) plain wholemeal flour

100 g (4 oz) Cheddar cheese, grated

75 g (3 oz) butter

1 Cook the leeks and peas in a little salted water in a tightly covered medium saucepan until tender. Drain well.
2 Purée the leeks, peas, milk and yogurt in a blender or food processor.
3 Beat 2 of the eggs into the purée and add salt and pepper to taste. Lightly beat the remaining egg in a small bowl.
4 Put the flour and half the cheese in a bowl. Rub in the butter until the mixture resembles fine breadcrumbs, then bind together with the remaining egg.
5 Roll out the pastry on a lightly floured surface and use to line a 23 cm (9 inch) flan dish. Pour in the leek mixture.
6 Sprinkle over the remaining cheese. Bake in the oven at 190°C (375°F) mark 5 for 50–55 minutes until golden.

To Freeze
Open freeze until solid, then overwrap in foil. Freeze for up to 3 months.

To Thaw and Serve
Thaw, unwrapped, on a wire rack at cool room temperature. Serve cold or reheat in the oven at 180°C (350°F) mark 4.

CAULIFLOWER CHEESE AND TOMATOES
A tangy variation of this favourite dish

SERVES 2

225 g (8 oz) cauliflower florets

salt

25 g (1 oz) plain wholemeal flour

25 g (1 oz) butter

300 ml (½ pint) milk

75 g (3 oz) Double Gloucester cheese, grated

10 ml (2 tsp) Worcestershire sauce

2 tomatoes, skinned and chopped

15 ml (1 tbsp) tomato chutney

1 Cook the cauliflower in a saucepan of boiling salted water for 10 minutes or until tender. Drain well.
2 Put the flour, butter and milk in a saucepan. Heat, whisking continuously, until the sauce thickens, boils and is smooth. Simmer for 2–3 minutes.
3 Remove the pan from the heat, add most of the cheese and stir until melted. Mix in the Worcestershire sauce.
4 Place the tomatoes and chutney in the base of a 750 ml (1¼ pint) flameproof dish. Cover with the cauliflower and cheese sauce.
5 Sprinkle with the remaining cheese and grill until bubbling and golden brown. Serve with brown bread.

To Freeze
Cool quickly at the end of step 4, then cover with double thickness foil and seal. Freeze for up to 2 months.

To Thaw and Serve
Reheat from frozen in the oven at 170°C (325°F) mark 3 for about 25–30 minutes. Complete as above.

VEGETARIAN ROAST

You can use any type of unsalted chopped nuts in this savoury loaf

SERVES 4–6

175 g (6 oz) long-grain brown rice

15 g (½ oz) butter

1 medium onion, skinned and chopped

1 garlic clove, skinned and crushed

2 carrots, peeled and grated

100 g (4 oz) button mushrooms, finely chopped

100 g (4 oz) fresh wholemeal breadcrumbs

100 g (4 oz) nuts, finely chopped

100 g (4 oz) mature Cheddar cheese, grated

2 eggs

salt and pepper

1 Cook the rice in a saucepan of boiling salted water for 30–35 minutes or until tender. Drain well.

2 Meanwhile, heat the butter in a medium frying pan, add the onion, garlic, carrots and mushrooms and fry, stirring frequently, until softened. Stir in the breadcrumbs, nuts, cooked rice, cheese and eggs. Add salt and pepper to taste and mix thoroughly together.

3 Pack the mixture into a greased 1.7 litre (3 pint) loaf tin. Bake in the oven at 180°C (350°F) mark 4 for 1–1¼ hours or until firm to the touch and brown on top. Serve sliced, hot or cold, with tomato sauce or chutney.

To Freeze

Cool, then overwrap in double thickness foil. Freeze for up to 3 months.

To Thaw and Serve

Thaw, loosely covered, overnight in the refrigerator. Serve cold or reheat in the oven at 180°C (350°F) mark 4 for about 20 minutes.

SPICY CHICK-PEAS AND SWEDE

The delicate flavour of swede makes an excellent background for nutty tasting chick-peas

SERVES 4

225 g (8 oz) dried chick-peas, soaked overnight

225 g (8 oz) swede, peeled and roughly chopped

salt and pepper

25 g (1 oz) butter

1 medium onion, skinned and roughly chopped

5 ml (1 tsp) cumin seeds

2.5 ml (½ tsp) dried oregano

10 ml (2 tsp) paprika

15 ml (1 tbsp) plain flour

450 g (1 lb) tomatoes, roughly chopped

50 g (2 oz) Cheddar cheese, grated

1 Drain the chick-peas and rinse under running cold water. Put in a large saucepan, cover with plenty of fresh cold water and slowly bring to the boil. Cover and simmer for 45 minutes or until just tender. Drain well.

2 Put the swede in a saucepan and cover with cold salted water. Bring to the boil, then simmer for 15–20 minutes or until tender. Drain, reserving 150 ml (¼ pint) cooking liquor.

3 Heat the butter in a medium saucepan, add the onion, cumin, oregano and paprika and fry for 1–2 minutes.

4 Stir in the flour. Cook, stirring, for 1–2 minutes, then gradually stir in the reserved liquor. Bring to the boil, then stir in the tomatoes. Cover and simmer for 2–3 minutes.

5 Add the chick-peas and swede and stir over a gentle heat for a few minutes until hot. Add salt and pepper to taste and serve, topped with a sprinkling of Cheddar cheese and accompanied by wholemeal bread.

To Freeze
At the end of step 4, put the chick-peas and swede into rigid containers and spoon over the sauce. Freeze for up to 1 month.

To Thaw and Serve
Thaw overnight in the refrigerator. Reheat in a heavy-based saucepan over moderate heat. Serve sprinkled with cheese.

TIAN A LA PROVENÇALE (AUBERGINE GRATIN)
Serve this creamy vegetable bake with jacket potatoes and a green salad for a satisfying supper

SERVES 4

450 g (1 lb) aubergines, thinly sliced

salt and pepper

25 g (1 oz) butter

25 g (1 oz) plain flour

300 ml (½ pint) milk

60 ml (4 tbsp) freshly grated Parmesan cheese

1.25 ml (¼ tsp) freshly grated nutmeg

about 150 ml (¼ pint) olive or vegetable oil

350 g (12 oz) tomatoes, skinned and sliced

2 garlic cloves, skinned and roughly chopped

2 eggs, beaten

1 Place the aubergine slices in a colander and sprinkle each layer with salt. Cover with a plate, place heavy weights on top and leave for 30 minutes.

2 Meanwhile, melt the butter in a saucepan, add the flour and cook gently, stirring, for 2 minutes. Remove from the heat and gradually blend in the milk. Bring to the boil, stirring constantly, then simmer for 3 minutes until thick and smooth. Add half of the cheese, the nutmeg and salt and pepper to taste, stir well to mix, then remove from the heat.

3 Rinse the aubergine slices under cold running water, then pat dry with absorbent kitchen paper.

4 Pour enough oil into a heavy-based frying pan to cover the base. Heat until very hot, then add a layer of aubergine slices. Fry over moderate heat until golden brown on both sides, turning once. Remove with a slotted spoon and drain on absorbent kitchen paper. Repeat with more oil and aubergines.

5 Arrange alternate layers of aubergines and tomatoes in an oiled gratin or baking dish. Sprinkle each layer with garlic, a little salt and plenty of pepper.

6 Beat the eggs into the sauce, then pour slowly into the dish. Sprinkle the remaining cheese evenly over the top. Bake in the oven at 200°C (400°F) mark 6 for 20 minutes or until golden brown and bubbling. Serve hot.

To Freeze
Before baking at step 6, open freeze until firm then wrap in foil. Freeze for up to 2 months.

To Thaw and Serve
Thaw overnight in the refrigerator. Cook in the oven at 200°C (400°F) mark 6 for 25–30 minutes.

DESSERTS

RHUBARB AND ORANGE FOOL
A lovely creamy dessert to make when
soft fruit is out of season

SERVES 6

450 g (1 lb) rhubarb

grated rind and juice of 1 orange

pinch of ground cinnamon

25–50 g (1–2 oz) sugar

300 ml (¹/₂ pint) whipping cream

5 ml (1 tsp) orange flower water or to taste

shredded orange rind, to decorate

1 Wipe the rhubarb and chop into 2.5 cm
(1 inch) pieces, discarding the leaves and
the white ends of the stalks.
2 Put the rhubarb, orange rind, juice,
cinnamon and sugar into a saucepan and
cook gently, covered, for about 15
minutes.
3 Remove the lid and boil rapidly for 10
minutes, stirring frequently, until the
mixture becomes a thick purée. Cool for
1 hour.
4 When cool, whip the cream until stiff.
Fold into the mixture with the orange
flower water to taste. Spoon into glasses
and chill for 1–2 hours until required.
Decorate with orange rind and serve with
sponge fingers.

To Freeze
Spoon the mousse into a freezerproof
dish at step 4 and overwrap. Freeze for up
to 3 months.

To Thaw and Serve
Thaw overnight in the refrigerator.
Decorate.

BAKED STRAWBERRY CHEESECAKE
For the fullest flavour make this
cheesecake when the strawberry season
is in full swing

SERVES 6–8

75 g (3 oz) self raising flour

25 g (1 oz) cornflour

75 g (3 oz) butter

milk, for mixing

100 g (4 oz) fresh strawberries, hulled and sliced

225 g (8 oz) medium-fat curd cheese

50 g (2 oz) caster sugar

2 eggs, separated

150 ml (¹/₄ pint) soured cream

1 Put the flour and cornflour in a bowl.
Rub in the butter until the mixture
resembles fine breadcrumbs, then add a
little milk to mix.
2 Roll out the dough on a lightly floured
surface and use to line a 23 cm (9 inch)
spring form tin. Bake blind in the oven at
200°C (400°F) mark 6 for 10 minutes
until set.
3 Arrange the strawberries in the pastry
case.
4 Blend together the cheese, sugar, egg
yolks and soured cream. Whisk the egg
whites until stiff and gently fold into the
mixture. Pour on top of the strawberries.
Bake at 180°C (350°F) mark 4 for 40–45
minutes until firm. Serve hot or cold.

To Freeze
Cool, then overwrap. Freeze for up to
1 month.

To Thaw and Serve
Thaw, wrapped, overnight in the
refrigerator.

SPICED APPLE AND PLUM CRUMBLE

A real taste of autumn in this spicy fruit crumble

SERVES 6
450 g (1 lb) plums
700 g (1½ lb) cooking apples
100 g (4 oz) butter
100 g (4 oz) sugar
7.5 ml (1½ tsp) ground mixed spice
175 g (6 oz) plain wholemeal flour
50 g (2 oz) blanched hazelnuts, toasted and chopped

1 Using a sharp knife, cut the plums in half and carefully remove the stones.
2 Peel, quarter, core and slice the apples. Place in a medium saucepan with 25 g (1 oz) of the butter, 50 g (2 oz) of the sugar and about 5 ml (1 tsp) mixed spice.
3 Cover and cook gently for 15 minutes until the apples begin to soften. Stir in the plums and turn into a 1.1 litre (2 pint) shallow ovenproof dish. Leave to cool for about 30 minutes.
4 Stir the flour and remaining mixed spice well together, then rub in the remaining butter until the mixture resembles fine breadcrumbs. Stir in the rest of the sugar with the hazelnuts.
5 Spoon the crumble mixture over the fruit. Bake in the oven at 180°C (350°F) mark 4 for about 40 minutes or until the top is golden, crisp and crumbly. Serve with cream.

To Freeze
Open freeze before baking at step 5, then overwrap. Freeze for up to 6 months.

To Thaw and Serve
Bake from frozen in the oven at 220°C (425°F) mark 7 for 15 minutes. Reduce the temperature to 180°C (350°F) mark 4 and bake for about 40 minutes.

WALNUT AND HONEY TART

This rich gooey tart is quite irresistible with it's nutty orange flavour

SERVES 6
175 g (6 oz) plain wholemeal flour
pinch of salt
75 g (3 oz) butter
finely grated rind and juice of 1 orange
60 ml (4 tbsp) clear honey
75 g (3 oz) fresh wholemeal breadcrumbs
45 ml (3 tbsp) dark soft brown sugar
3 eggs
100 g (4 oz) walnut pieces, roughly chopped

1 To make the pastry, put the flour and salt in a bowl and rub in the butter until the mixture resembles fine breadcrumbs. Stir in the orange rind and enough orange juice to bind the mixture together.
2 Roll out the dough on a lightly floured surface and use to line a 20.5 cm (8 inch) fluted flan dish or tin. Bake blind in the oven at 200°C (400°F) mark 6 for 10–15 minutes until set.
3 Mix the honey, breadcrumbs and sugar together. Gradually beat in the eggs, one at a time, and any remaining orange juice.
4 Sprinkle the walnuts in the bottom of the pastry case and pour over the filling. Bake for 20–25 minutes until set. Cover the tart with greaseproof paper if it browns too quickly. Serve warm or cold with clotted or double cream.

To Freeze
Open freeze until solid, then overwrap in foil. Freeze for up to 3 months.

To Thaw and Serve
Place on a baking sheet in the foil wrapping and cook in the oven at 200°C (400°F) mark 6 for 20 minutes. Uncover and cook 5–10 minutes more.

MANDARIN AND LYCHEE MOUSSE

SERVES 6

3 eggs, separated

2 egg yolks

75 g (3 oz) caster sugar

298 (10½ oz) can mandarin oranges

310 g (11 oz) can lychees in syrup

15 ml (3 tsp) powdered gelatine

150 ml (¼ pint) double cream

1 Put the 5 yolks and sugar in a large heatproof bowl and stand over a pan of gently simmering water. Whisk until thick and holds a ribbon trail, then remove from the pan. Leave for 30 minutes, whisking occasionally.
2 Reserve 60 ml (4 tbsp) of the mandarin juice. Purée half the oranges and the remaining juice in a blender with the lychees and half the syrup.
3 Put the reserved mandarin syrup in a heatproof bowl and sprinkle in the gelatine. Stand the bowl over a pan of hot water and heat until dissolved. Remove from the pan and cool slightly.
4 Stir the mandarin and lychee purée into the cooled egg yolk mixture, then stir in the gelatine liquid until evenly mixed.
5 Whip the cream until standing in soft peaks. Whisk the egg whites until stiff. Fold first the cream and then the egg whites into the mousse. Turn into a glass serving bowl and chill until set.
6 When the mousse is set, serve decorated with the reserved mandarin oranges and extra whipped cream.

To Freeze
Turn into a freezerproof dish at step 5 and overwrap. Freeze for up to 3 months.

To Thaw and Serve
Thaw overnight in the refrigerator. Decorate.

ALMOND AND CHERRY FLAN

For a variation on this recipe, replace the cherries with well drained canned apricot halves

SERVES 6

225 g (8 oz) plain flour

225 g (8 oz) butter

50 g (2 oz) self raising flour

2.5 ml (½ tsp) baking powder

2 eggs, separated

350 g (12 oz) fresh ripe black cherries, stoned

50 g (2 oz) caster sugar

100 g (4 oz) ground almonds

5 ml (1 tsp) almond flavouring

15 ml (1 tbsp) almond-flavoured liqueur (optional)

50 g (2 oz) self raising flour

2.5 ml (½ tsp) baking powder

45 ml (3 tbsp) milk

25 g (1 oz) flaked almonds

1 Place the plain flour in a large bowl and rub in 175 g (6 oz) of the butter until the mixture resembles fine breadcrumbs. Bind to a firm dough with 1 egg yolk mixed with 30–45 ml (2–3 tbsp) water.
2 Roll out the dough on a lightly floured surface and use to line a 24 cm (9½ inch) flan dish. Bake blind in the oven at 200°C (400°F) mark 6 for 15–20 minutes until set but not browned; cool slightly.
3 Scatter the cherries over the pastry. Cream the remaining butter and sugar well together and beat in the ground almonds with the almond flavouring, liqueur, if using, and the remaining egg yolk. Sift together the self raising flour and baking powder, then fold into the almond mixture. Lightly stir in the milk.
4 Whisk the 2 eggs whites until stiff, then fold them into the creamed ingredients.
5 Spread the almond mixture over the cherries in the flan case and scatter the

flaked almonds on top. Bake at 180°C (350°F) mark 4 for about 30 minutes.

To Freeze
Cool, then overwrap. Freeze for up to 3 months.

To Thaw and Serve
Thaw at cool room temperature. Reheat in the oven at 180°C (350°F) mark 4 for 15–20 minutes.

RASPBERRY AND REDCURRANT FREEZE

The tangy fruit flavour of this ice makes a stunning dessert for dinner parties

SERVES 4–6
350 g (12 oz) fresh or frozen raspberries
225 g (8 oz) jar redcurrant jelly
300 ml (½ pint) soured cream

1 Put the raspberries and redcurrant jelly in a saucepan and heat gently, stirring frequently, until the fruit is soft. Transfer to a blender or food processor and work to a purée. Sieve to remove the seeds. Chill for about 1 hour until cold.
2 Whisk in the soured cream, then pour into a freezerproof container (not metal) at least 5 cm (2 inches) deep. Freeze for about 2 hours until firm but not hard.
3 Turn the frozen mixture into a bowl and break into pieces. Beat until smooth, creamy and lighter in colour. Return to the freezer container and freeze for a further 2 hours until firm.
4 Allow to soften slightly in the refrigerator for about 1 hour before serving with small crisp biscuits.

To Freeze
Freeze for up to 3 months at step 3.

To Thaw and Serve
As step 4.

COFFEENUT ICE CREAM

SERVES 4
100 g (4 oz) hazelnuts
50 ml (2 tbsp plus 4 tsp) coffee-flavoured liqueur
15 ml (1 tbsp) coffee and chicory essence
300 ml (½ pint) double cream
300 ml (½ pint) single cream
75 g (3 oz) icing sugar, sifted

1 Toast the hazelnuts under the grill for a few minutes, shaking the grill pan constantly so that the nuts brown evenly.
2 Tip the nuts into a clean tea-towel and rub to remove the skins. Chop finely.
3 Mix 30 ml (2 tbsp) of the coffee liqueur and the essence together in a bowl. Stir in the chopped nuts, reserving a few for decoration.
4 In a separate bowl, whip the creams and icing sugar together until thick. Fold in the nut mixture, then turn into a shallow freezerproof container. Freeze for 2 hours until ice crystals form around the edge of the ice cream.
5 Turn the ice cream into a bowl and beat thoroughly for a few minutes to break up the ice crystals. Return to the freezer container, cover and freeze for at least 4 hours, preferably overnight (to allow enough time for the flavours to develop).
6 To serve, transfer the ice cream to the refrigerator for 30 minutes to soften slightly, then scoop into individual glasses. Spoon 5 ml (1 tsp) coffee liqueur over each serving and sprinkle with the remaining nuts. Serve immediately.

To Freeze
Freeze for up to 3 months at step 5.

To Thaw and Serve
As step 6.

BANANA CHEESECAKE

SERVES 6–8

225 g (8 oz) ginger biscuits
100 g (4 oz) butter, melted and cooled
225 g (8 oz) full fat soft cheese
150 ml (¼ pint) soured cream
3 bananas
30 ml (2 tbsp) clear honey
15 ml (1 tbsp) chopped preserved ginger (with syrup)
15 ml (3 tsp) powdered gelatine
60 ml (4 tbsp) lemon juice
banana slices and preserved ginger slices

1 To make the biscuit crust, crush the biscuits finely in a bowl with the end of a rolling pin. Stir in the melted butter.
2 Press the mixture over the base of a 20.5 cm (8 inch) springform tin or deep cake tin with a removable base. Chill.
3 Beat the cheese and cream together until well mixed. Peel and mash the bananas, then beat into the cheese mixture with the honey and ginger.
4 Sprinkle the gelatine over the lemon juice in a small heatproof bowl. Stand the bowl over a saucepan of hot water and heat gently until dissolved.
5 Stir the dissolved gelatine slowly into the cheesecake mixture, then spoon into the biscuit-lined tin. Chill for about 3–4 hours until the mixture is set.
6 To serve, remove the cheesecake carefully from the tin and place on a serving plate. Decorate around the edge with banana and ginger slices. Serve as soon as possible.

To Freeze
Open freeze at step 5 until firm and overwrap. Freeze for up to 2 months.

To Thaw and Serve
Thaw overnight in the refrigerator. Complete step 6.

SQUIDGY CHOCOLATE ROLL

SERVES 6–8

60 ml (4 tbsp) cocoa powder
150 ml (¼ pint) milk
4 eggs, separated
100 g (4 oz) caster sugar
225 ml (8 fl oz) double cream
fresh strawberries and grated chocolate

1 Grease and line a 20.5 x 30.5 cm (8 x 12 inch) Swiss roll tin. Mix the cocoa powder and milk in a small saucepan and heat gently until the cocoa powder has dissolved. Set aside to cool.
2 Whisk the egg yolks and sugar together in a bowl until pale and fluffy. Whisk the cooled milk mixture into the egg yolk mixture.
3 Whisk the egg whites until stiff, then fold into the cocoa mixture. Spread the mixture evenly into the prepared tin.
4 Bake in the oven at 180°C (350°F) mark 4 for about 20 minutes until the sponge has risen and is just firm to the touch. Turn out on to a sheet of greaseproof paper and cover with a warm, damp tea-towel to prevent the sponge from drying out. Cool for 20 minutes.
5 Meanwhile, whip the cream until stiff. Spread over the sponge, reserving half for decorating and then roll it up carefully. Do not roll up too tightly and do not worry if it cracks slightly. Pipe the reserved cream on top and decorate with strawberries and grated chocolate. Chill.

To Freeze
Open freeze before decorating at step 5, then wrap in foil. Freeze for up to 4 months.

To Thaw and Serve
Thaw, unwrapped, at cool room temperature. Decorate and chill until ready to serve.

BLACKBERRY AND PEAR COBBLER

A border of overlapping scones makes a satisfying fruit pudding

SERVES 4

450 g (1 lb) blackberries

450 g (1 lb) ripe cooking pears, such as Conference

finely grated rind and juice of 1 lemon

2.5 ml (½ tsp) ground cinnamon

225 g (8 oz) self raising flour

pinch of salt

50 g (2 oz) butter

25 g (1 oz) caster sugar

about 150 ml (¼ pint) milk, plus extra

1 Pick over the blackberries and wash. Peel and core the pears, then slice thickly.
2 Put the blackberries and pears into a saucepan with the lemon rind and juice and the cinnamon. Poach gently for 15–20 minutes until the fruit is juicy and tender.
3 Meanwhile, place the flour and salt into the bowl. Rub in the butter, then stir in the sugar. Gradually add the milk to mix to a fairly soft dough.
4 Roll out the dough on a lightly floured surface until 1.5 cm (½ inch) thick. Cut out rounds using a fluted 5 cm (2 inch) pastry cutter.
5 Put the fruit in a pie dish and top with overlapping pastry rounds, leaving a gap in the centre. Brush the top of the pastry rounds with milk. Bake in the oven at 220°C (425°F) mark 7 for 10–15 minutes until the pastry is golden brown.

To Freeze
Cool, then overwrap. Freeze for up to 2 months.

To Thaw and Serve
Thaw at cool room temperature. Cook in the oven at 190°C (375°F) mark 5 for 15–20 minutes.

ORANGE SHERBET

Serve this refreshing iced dessert after a rich main course

SERVES 8

178 ml (6¼ oz) carton frozen orange juice

175 g (6 oz) caster sugar

45 ml (3 tbsp) golden syrup

45 ml (3 tbsp) lemon juice

568 ml (1 pint) milk

300 ml (½ pint) single cream

shreds of orange rind and mint sprigs, to decorate

1 Tip the frozen, undiluted orange juice into a deep bowl. Leave until beginning to soften, then add the sugar, golden syrup and lemon juice. Whisk until smooth.
2 Combine the orange mixture with the milk and cream and pour into a deep, rigid, freezerproof container. Cover and freeze for 4–5 hours. There is no need to whisk the mixture during freezing.
3 Transfer to the refrigerator to soften 45 minutes – 1 hour before serving. Serve scooped into individual glasses or orange shells, decorated with orange shreds and mint sprigs.

To Freeze
Freeze for up to 3 months at step 2.

To Thaw and Serve
As step 3.

BAKING

HERBY CHEESE LOAF

This quick and easy bread is ideal to
serve with soup

MAKES ONE 450 G (1 LB) LOAF

225 g (8 oz) self raising flour

7.5 ml (1½ tsp) salt

5 ml (1 tsp) mustard powder

5 ml (1 tsp) snipped fresh chives

15 ml (1 tbsp) chopped fresh parsley

75 g (3 oz) mature Cheddar cheese, grated

1 egg, beaten

25 g (1 oz) butter, melted

1 Grease a 900 ml (1½ pint) loaf tin. Sift
the flour, salt and mustard into a bowl and
stir in the herbs and cheese.
2 Add the egg, 150 ml (¼ pint) water
and melted butter, then stir until well
blended with a wooden spoon. Spoon the
mixture into the prepared loaf tin.
3 Bake in the oven at 190°C (375°F)
mark 5 for about 45 minutes. Turn out
and cool on a wire rack for about 1 hour.
Serve sliced and buttered while warm.

To Freeze
Cool, then overwrap. Freeze for up to 1
month.

To Thaw and Serve
Unwrap and return to the tin. Reheat in
the oven at 200°C (400°F) mark 6 for
15–20 minutes until heated through.

SODA BREAD

This moist, close-textured bread was
traditionally baked on a griddle over an
open fire

MAKES 1 LARGE LOAF

450 g (1 lb) plain wholemeal flour

100 g (4 oz) plain flour

50 g (2 oz) rolled oats

5 ml (1 tsp) bicarbonate of soda

5 ml (1 tsp) salt

about 450 ml (¾ pint) buttermilk

1 Grease a baking sheet. Put the flours,
oats, bicarbonate of soda and salt in a
large bowl and mix together. Add enough
buttermilk to mix to a soft dough.
2 Knead very lightly, then shape into a
large round and place on the prepared
baking sheet. Cut a deep cross in the top.
3 Bake in the oven at 230°C (450°F)
mark 8 for 15 minutes, then reduce the
oven temperature to 200°C (400°F) mark
6 and bake for a further 20–25 minutes or
until the loaf sounds hollow when tapped
on the bottom. Eat while still warm.

To Freeze
Cool, then overwrap. Freeze for up to 3
months.

To Thaw and Serve
Thaw, unwrapped, at cool room
temperature.

PRUNE AND NUT TEABREAD

SERVES 8–10

275 g (10 oz) self raising flour
pinch of salt
7.5 ml (1½ tsp) ground cinnamon
75 g (3 oz) butter, cut into pieces
75 g (3 oz) demerara sugar
1 egg, beaten
100 ml (4 fl oz) milk
50 g (2 oz) walnuts, chopped
100 g (4 oz) stoned tenderised prunes
15 ml (1 tbsp) clear honey

1 Grease a 2 litre (3½ pint) loaf tin. Base-line the tin and grease the paper.
2 Sift the flour and salt into a bowl and add the cinnamon. Rub in the butter until the mixture resembles fine breadcrumbs.
3 Stir in the sugar and make a well in the centre. Add the egg and milk and gradually draw in the dry ingredients to form a smooth dough.
4 Using floured hands, shape the mixture into 16 rounds. Place 8 in the base of the tin. Sprinkle over half the nuts.
5 Snip the prunes and sprinkle on top of the nuts. Place the remaining dough rounds on top and sprinkle over the remaining chopped walnuts.
6 Bake in the oven at 190°C (375°F) mark 5 for about 50 minutes or until firm to the touch. Check near the end of cooking time and cover if overbrowning.
7 Turn out on to a wire rack to cool for 1 hour. When cold, brush with the honey to glaze. Wrap and store for 1–2 days in an airtight tin before slicing and buttering.

To Freeze
Cool, then overwrap before glazing. Freeze for up to 3 months.

To Thaw and Serve
Thaw, unwrapped, at cool room temperature. Glaze with honey.

SPICED WALNUT SCONES

MAKES 16

100 g (4 oz) plain wholemeal flour
100 g (4 oz) plain white flour
15 ml (1 tbsp) baking powder
2.5 ml (½ tsp) ground mixed spice
pinch of salt
50 g (2 oz) butter
15 ml (1 tbsp) caster sugar
75 g (3 oz) walnut pieces, roughly chopped
10 ml (2 tsp) lemon juice
200 ml (7 fl oz) milk
honey and chopped walnuts, to decorate

1 Sift the flours into a bowl with the baking powder, mixed spice and salt. Stir in the bran left in the bottom of the sieve. Rub in the butter. Stir in the sugar and 50 g (2 oz) of the walnuts.
2 Mix the lemon juice with 170 ml (6 fl oz) of the milk and stir into the dry ingredients until evenly mixed.
3 Turn out the dough on to a lightly floured surface and knead lightly.
4 Roll out the dough to a 20.5 cm (8 inch) square and place on a baking sheet. Mark the surface into 16 squares, cutting through to a depth of 3 mm (⅛ inch).
5 Lightly brush the dough with the remaining milk, then sprinkle over the remaining chopped walnut pieces.
6 Bake in the oven at 220°C (425°F) mark 7 for about 18 minutes or until well risen, golden brown and firm to the touch. Cut into squares. Serve warm, brushed with honey.

To Freeze
Cool, wrap in foil and overwrap. Freeze for up to 3 months.

To Thaw and Serve
Remove the polythene bag and place the foil package on a baking sheet. Reheat in the oven at 180°C (350°F) mark 4 for 10–12 minutes.

POPPY SEED ROLLS

MAKES 8

15 g (½ oz) fresh yeast or 7.5 ml (1½ tsp) dried

325 ml (11 fl oz) tepid milk

450 g (1 lb) strong white flour

45 ml (3 tbsp) poppy seeds

5 ml (1 tsp) salt

5 ml (1 tsp) sugar

beaten egg and milk, to glaze

1 Blend the fresh yeast with the milk. If using dried yeast, sprinkle it on to the milk and leave in a warm place for 15 minutes or until frothy.

2 Mix the flour, 30 ml (2 tbsp) of the poppy seeds, the salt and sugar together in a bowl. Pour in the yeast mixture and mix well to form a firm dough.

3 Turn out the dough on to a floured surface and knead for at least 10 minutes until smooth and elastic. Place in an oiled bowl, cover with oiled polythene and leave in a warm place until doubled in size.

4 Knead the dough again for 5 minutes. Divide into 24 pieces. Shape each piece into a ball. On a floured baking sheet, place the dough balls in triangular groups of three. Cover with oiled polythene and leave in a warm place until risen.

5 Brush with a mixture of beaten egg and milk. Sprinkle with the remaining poppy seeds. Bake in the oven at 200°C (400°F) mark 6 for about 20 minutes. Cool on a wire rack.

To Freeze

Cool, wrap in a single layer in foil and overwrap. Freeze for up to 3 months.

To Thaw and Serve

Remove the polythene bag and place the foil package on a baking sheet. Reheat in the oven at 180°C (350°F) mark 4 for 10–12 minutes.

QUICK PEANUT LOAF

MAKES TWO 450 G (1 LB) LOAVES

15 g (½ oz) fresh yeast or 7.5 ml (1½ tsp) dried and 5 ml (1 tsp) sugar

450 g (1 lb) strong plain white flour

5 ml (1 tsp) salt

60 ml (4 tbsp) crunchy peanut butter

milk, to glaze

sea salt

1 Lightly grease two 900 ml (1½ pint) loaf tins. Dissolve the fresh yeast in 325 ml (11 fl oz) tepid water. If using dried yeast, sprinkle it on to the water with the sugar and leave in a warm place for 15 minutes or until frothy.

2 Place the flour and salt in a bowl, then using a fork 'cut' in the peanut butter. Make a well in the centre and pour in the yeast liquid and mix to a soft dough.

3 Turn out on to a lightly floured surface and knead for about 10 minutes until smooth and no longer sticky.

4 Divide the dough in two and knead into oblong shapes to fit the tins. Place the dough seam-side down in the prepared tins. Cover loosely with oiled polythene and leave in a warm place for about 1 hour or until doubled in size.

5 Using a large sharp knife, make a shallow cut along each loaf. Brush with milk and sprinkle over a little sea salt.

6 Bake in the oven at 230°C (450°F) mark 8 for about 20 minutes or until well risen, golden brown and hollow-sounding when tapped on the bottom. Cool on a wire rack.

To Freeze

Cool, then overwrap. Freeze for up to 2 months.

To Thaw and Serve

Thaw, wrapped, at cool room temperature.

BATH BUNS

This light, sugary bun dates back to 18th century Bath, where it is still sold in the Pump Room

MAKES ABOUT 18

25 g (1 oz) fresh yeast or 15 ml (1 tbsp) dried

150 ml (¼ pint) tepid milk

450 g (1 lb) strong white flour

5 ml (1 tsp) salt

50 g (2 oz) caster sugar

50 g (2 oz) butter, melted and cooled

2 eggs, beaten

175 g (6 oz) sultanas

30–45 ml (2–3 tbsp) chopped mixed peel

beaten egg, to glaze

crushed sugar lumps, to decorate

1 Grease 2 baking sheets. Blend the fresh yeast with the milk and 60 ml (4 tbsp) tepid water. If using dried yeast, sprinkle it on to the milk and water and leave in a warm place for 15 minutes or until frothy.
2 Sift the flour and salt together in a bowl and add the sugar. Make a well in the centre and stir in the butter, eggs, yeast mixture, sultanas and peel and mix well. The dough should be fairly soft.
3 Turn the dough on to a floured surface and knead until smooth. Place in an oiled bowl, cover with oiled polythene and leave in a warm place for about 1 hour or until doubled in size.
4 Knead the dough well. Divide into 18 pieces, roll each into a ball and place on the prepared baking sheets. Cover with oiled polythene and leave in a warm place for about 1 hour or until doubled in size.
5 Brush the dough with egg and sprinkle with crushed sugar. Bake in the oven at 190°C (375°F) mark 5 for about 15 minutes until golden brown. Cool on a wire rack and serve buttered.

To Freeze
Cool, then pack in a single layer in rigid containers. Freeze for up to 3 months.

To Thaw and Serve
Place the frozen buns on a baking sheet and cover with foil. Reheat in the oven at 200°C (400°F) mark 6 for about 20 minutes until warmed through.

ORANGE TEABREAD

Use the juice from sweet oranges, clementines or satsumas

MAKES 10–12 SLICES

50 g (2 oz) butter

175 g (6 oz) caster sugar

1 egg, beaten

finely grated rind of 1 orange

30 ml (2 tbsp) orange juice

30 ml (2 tbsp) milk

225 g (8 oz) plain flour

12.5 ml (2½ tsp) baking powder

1 Grease a 1.3 litre (2¼ pint) loaf tin and line with greaseproof paper.
2 Cream the butter and sugar together in a bowl until pale and fluffy. Gradually beat in the egg. Slowly add the orange rind and juice: it does not matter if the mixture curdles. Lightly beat in the milk alternately with the sifted flour and baking powder.
3 Turn the mixture into the prepared tin. Bake in the oven at 190°C (375°F) mark 5 for 40–50 minutes or until well risen and firm to the touch. Cool on a wire rack.

To Freeze
Cool, then overwrap. Freeze for up to 4 months.

To Thaw and Serve
Thaw, wrapped, at cool room temperature.

GRANARY BREAD

Granary flour is a strong brown flour with added cracked wheat which gives a nutty flavour.

MAKES 2 LARGE LOAVES

450 g (1 lb) granary flour

175 g (6 oz) strong white plain flour

7.5 ml (1½ tsp) salt

25 g (1 oz) butter

25 g (1 oz) fresh yeast or 15 ml (1 tbsp) dried and 5 ml (1 tsp) sugar

15 ml (1 tbsp) malt extract

1 Grease two 1.3 litre (2¼ pint) loaf tins. Mix the flours and salt in a bowl and rub in the butter.

2 Cream the fresh yeast with the malt extract and 150 ml (¼ pint) tepid water and add to the flour with a further 250 ml (9 fl oz) tepid water. If using dried yeast, sprinkle it on to the 150 ml (¼ pint) water with the sugar, add the malt extract and a further 250 ml (9 fl oz) tepid water, then leave in a warm place for 15 minutes or until frothy.

3 Add the yeast mixture to the flour and butter mixture, then mix to a soft dough. Turn on to a floured surface and knead for 10 minutes until firm, elastic and no longer sticky. Place in an oiled bowl and cover with oiled polythene. Leave to rise in a warm place until doubled in size.

4 Turn out the dough on to a lightly floured surface and knead for 2–3 minutes. Divide into 2 pieces and knead each piece until smooth and elastic. Shape into oblongs and place in the prepared tins. Cover with oiled polythene and leave in a warm place until the dough is 1 cm (½ inch) above the top of the tins.

5 Bake in the oven at 220°C (425°F) mark 7 for 30–35 minutes or until well risen and hollow-sounding when tapped on the bottom. Cover lightly with greaseproof paper if browning too quickly. Cool on a wire rack.

To Freeze

Cool, then overwrap. Freeze for up to 6 months.

To Thaw and Serve

Thaw, unwrapped, at cool room temperature.

MAIDSTONE BISCUITS

Buy rose water from the chemist for the these authentic Tudor biscuits

MAKES ABOUT 18

100 g (4 oz) butter

100 g (4 oz) caster sugar

150 g (5 oz) plain flour

5 ml (1 tsp) rose water

50 g (2 oz) blanched almonds, chopped

1 Flour a baking sheet. Cream the butter and sugar together in a bowl until pale and fluffy.

2 Fold in the flour, rose water and almonds, then mix to make a stiff dough. Place in small heaps on the prepared baking sheet.

3 Bake in the oven at 180°C (350°F) mark 4 for 12–15 minutes until golden brown. Cool on a wire rack. Store in an airtight container.

To Freeze

Cool, then pack into a rigid container. Freeze for up to 3 months.

To Thaw and Serve

Thaw, wrapped, at cool room temperature.

DUNDEE CAKE

The classic rich, buttery fruit cake –
named after the town where the recipe
originated

MAKES ABOUT 16 SLICES

100 g (4 oz) currants
100 g (4 oz) seedless raisins
100 g (4 oz) sultanas
100 g (4 oz) chopped candied orange peel
25 g (1 oz) blanched almonds, chopped
275 g (10 oz) plain flour
225 g (8 oz) butter
225 g (8 oz) light soft brown sugar
finely grated rind of 1 orange
finely grated rind of 1 lemon
4 eggs
whole blanched almonds, to decorate

1 Grease and line a deep 20.5 cm (8 inch)
round cake tin with greaseproof paper.
Mix the fruit, peel and chopped almonds
with the flour.
2 Cream the butter, sugar and orange
and lemon rinds together in bowl until
pale and fluffy. Gradually beat in the eggs.
3 Fold in the fruit and flour mixture,
then spoon into the prepared tin. Make a
slight hollow in the centre of the top.
Arrange whole almonds in circles to
decorate.
4 Bake in the oven at 170°C (325°F)
mark 3 for 2½–3 hours or until firm to the
touch. If the top gets too brown, cover
with paper. Leave to cool in the tin for 30
minutes, then turn on to a wire rack.

To Freeze
Cool, then overwrap. Freeze for up to 4
months.

To Thaw and Serve
Thaw, loosely covered, at cool room
temperature.

SOMERSET APPLE CAKE

This deliciously moist cake is equally
good served with cream as a pudding

MAKES ABOUT 10 SLICES

100 g (4 oz) butter
175 g (6 oz) dark soft brown sugar
2 eggs, beaten
225 g (8 oz) plain wholemeal flour
5 ml (1 tsp) ground mixed spice
5 ml (1 tsp) ground cinnamon
10 ml (2 tsp) baking powder
*450 g (1 lb) cooking apples, peeled, cored
and chopped*
45–60 ml (3–4 tbsp) milk
15 ml (1 tbsp) clear honey
*15 ml (1 tbsp) light demerara sugar, to
decorate*

1 Grease and line a deep 18 cm (7 inch)
round cake tin. Cream the butter and
sugar together in a bowl until pale and
fluffy.
2 Add the eggs, a little at a time, beating
well after each addition. Stir in the flour,
spices and baking powder and mix well.
Fold in the apples and enough milk to
make a soft dropping consistency.
3 Turn the mixture into the prepared tin.
Bake in the oven at 170°C (325°F) mark 3
for 1½ hours until well risen and firm to
the touch. Turn out on to a wire rack to
cool.
4 When the cake is cold, brush with the
honey and sprinkle with the demerara
sugar to decorate.

To Freeze
Cool at step 3, then overwrap. Freeze for
up to 3 months.

To Thaw and Serve
Thaw, wrapped, at cool room
temperature. Complete step 4.

BROWN SUGAR WHEATMEALS
Oats and currants provide contrast in these crunchy little ring biscuits

MAKES ABOUT 20

175 g (6 oz) plain wheatmeal flour
1.25 ml (¼ tsp) bicarbonate of soda
1.25 ml (¼ tsp) salt
50 g (2 oz) light soft brown sugar
75 g (3 oz) butter, cut into pieces
100 g (4 oz) currants
50 g (2 oz) oatflakes
1 egg, beaten

1 Grease 2 baking sheets. Place the flour, bicarbonate of soda, salt and sugar into a bowl. Rub in the butter until the mixture resembles fine breadcrumbs.
2 Stir in the currants and oatflakes, then stir in the beaten egg and just enough water, about 15 ml (1 tbsp), to bind the mixture together. Knead in the bowl until smooth. Cover and refrigerate for 20 minutes.
3 Roll out the dough on a lightly floured surface to about 0.5 cm (¼ inch) thickness. Cut into rounds with a 6.5 cm (2½ inch) fluted cutter and remove the centres with a 2.5 cm (1 inch) round cutter.
4 Carefully transfer the rings to the prepared baking sheets. Re-roll trimmings as necessary. Chill for at least 20 minutes.
5 Bake in the oven at 190°C (375°F) mark 5 for about 15 minutes until firm. Transfer to a wire rack to cool for 30 minutes.

To Freeze
Cool, then pack into a rigid container. Freeze for up to 3 months.

To Thaw and Serve
Thaw, wrapped, at cool room temperature.

GINGERBREAD MEN

MAKES ABOUT 16

350 g (12 oz) plain flour
5 ml (1 tsp) bicarbonate of soda
10 ml (2 tsp) ground ginger
100 g (4 oz) butter, diced
175 g (6 oz) soft light brown sugar
60 ml (4 tbsp) golden syrup
1 egg, beaten
currants, to decorate

1 Grease 3–4 baking sheets. Sift the flour, bicarbonate of soda and ginger into a bowl. Rub in the butter until the mixture resembles fine breadcrumbs, then stir in the sugar. Beat the syrup into the egg, then stir into the flour mixture. Mix together to make a smooth dough.
2 Knead the dough until smooth, then divide in half. Roll out, half at a time, on a lightly floured surface until about 0.5 cm (¼ inch) thick.
3 Using a gingerbread man cutter, cut out gingerbread men until all of the dough has been used, re-rolling and cutting the trimmings. Repeat with the second half of dough. Place the gingerbread men on the prepared baking sheets and decorate them with currants, to represent eyes and buttons.
4 Bake in the oven at 190°C (375°F) mark 5 for 12–15 minutes until golden brown. Leave on the baking sheets to cool slightly, then transfer carefully to wire racks and leave to cool completely. Store the gingerbread men in an airtight container.

To Freeze
Cool, then pack into rigid containers. Freeze for up to 4 months.

To Thaw and Serve
Thaw, wrapped, at cool room temperature.

APRICOT CRUNCH

Wholesome and crunchy wedges of oats and muesli make a good contribution to lunchbox meals

MAKES 16 WEDGES

75 g (3 oz) dried apricots
100 g (4 oz) butter
100 g (4 oz) demerara sugar
75 ml (5 tbsp) golden syrup
200 g (7 oz) crunchy toasted muesli cereal
150 g (5 oz) rolled oats
2.5 ml (½ tsp) ground mixed spice
10 ml (2 tsp) lemon juice

1 Base-line two 18 cm (7 inch) round sandwich tins with greaseproof paper.
2 Simmer the apricots gently in 200 ml (⅓ pint) water for about 10 minutes or until softened. Purée the apricots and cooking liquid in a blender or food processor until smooth. Cool for about 1 hour.
3 Slowly melt the butter, sugar and syrup. Stir in the cereal and oats and continue stirring until thoroughly combined. Add the puréed apricots, mixed spice and lemon juice. Mix well.
4 Divide the mixture between the prepared tins and spread evenly over the base. Press down well to level the surface.
5 Bake in the oven at 180°C (350°F) mark 4 for about 35 minutes. Cut each round into 8 wedges. Cool in the tins for 30 minutes until firm. Carefully ease the wedges out of the tins and store in an airtight container when completely cold.

To Freeze
Cool, then pack into a rigid container or overwrap in wedges. Freeze for up to 2 months.

To Thaw and Serve
Thaw, wrapped, at cool room temperature.

FIG SLY CAKES

Named 'sly' because a rich filling hides inside the plain pastry wrapping

MAKES 12

275 g (10 oz) plain flour
pinch of salt
100 g (4 oz) butter, diced
75 g (3 oz) lard, diced
50 g (2 oz) caster sugar
225 g (8 oz) dried figs, chopped
75 g (3 oz) walnut pieces, chopped
50 g (2 oz) currants
50 g (2 oz) raisins
milk, to glaze

1 To make the pastry, put the flour and salt into a bowl, then rub in the butter and lard until the mixture resembles fine breadcrumbs. Stir in the sugar and enough water to bind the mixture together. Chill while preparing the filling.
2 Put the figs, walnuts, currants and raisins into a saucepan with 150 ml (¼ pint) water. Cook, uncovered, stirring, until the water has evaporated and the mixture is soft and thick. Cool.
3 Divide the dough in half. Roll out one half to fit a shallow 18 × 28 cm (7 × 11 inch) tin. Spread the fruit mixture over the dough, then roll out the remaining dough and use to cover the filling. Seal the edges well and mark into 12 squares. Brush the top with a little milk to glaze.
4 Bake in the oven at 190°C (375°F) mark 5 for about 40 minutes until golden brown. Cool, then cut into the squares.

To Freeze
Cool, then pack into rigid containers, interleaving with greaseproof paper. Freeze for up to 3 months.

To Thaw and Serve
Thaw in the containers at cool room temperature.

LEMON SWISS ROLL

SERVES 6–8

3 eggs, size 2

100 g (4 oz) caster sugar

100 g (4 oz) plain flour

150 ml (¼ pint) double cream

about 275 g (10 oz) lemon curd

100 g (4 oz) icing sugar, sifted

1 Grease a 33×23×1 cm (13×9×½ inch) Swiss roll tin. Line the base with greaseproof paper and grease the paper. Dust with caster sugar and flour.
2 Whisk the eggs and sugar in a bowl until thick enough to leave a trail on the surface when the whisk is lifted. Sift in the flour and fold in gently.
3 Turn the mixture into the prepared tin and level the surface. Bake in the oven at 200°C (400°F) mark 6 for 10–12 minutes or until the cake springs back when pressed lightly with a finger.
4 Sugar a sheet of greaseproof paper and turn out the cake on to it. Roll up with the paper inside. Cool on a wire rack.
5 Whip the cream until it just holds its shape. Unroll the Swiss roll and spread with three-quarters of the lemon curd. Top with cream, then roll up again and place on a serving plate.
6 Make a glacé icing with the icing sugar and 20 ml (4 tsp) water. Spoon the icing on to the Swiss roll. Immediately, using the point of a teaspoon, draw rough lines of lemon curd across the icing and pull a skewer through to form a feather pattern. Leave to set for about 1 hour.

To Freeze
Cool, then overwrap at step 4. Freeze for up to 2 months.

To Thaw and Serve
Thaw, wrapped, at cool room temperature. Complete steps 5–6.

CHERRY AND COCONUT CAKE
Coconut gives a sweet nutty flavour to this family loaf cake

SERVES 8–10

250 g (9 oz) self raising flour

1.25 ml (¼ tsp) salt

125 g (4 oz) butter, cut into pieces

75 g (3 oz) desiccated coconut

125 g (4 oz) caster sugar

125 g (4 oz) glacé cherries, finely chopped

2 eggs, size 6, beaten

225 ml (8 fl oz) milk

25 g (1 oz) shredded coconut

1 Grease a 1.3 litre (2¼ pint) loaf tin. Base-line with greaseproof paper, grease the paper and dust with flour.
2 Put the flour and salt into a bowl and rub in the butter until the mixture resembles fine breadcrumbs. Stir in the coconut, sugar and cherries.
3 Whisk together the eggs and milk and beat into the dry ingredients. Turn the mixture into the tin, level the surface and scatter over the shredded coconut.
4 Bake in the oven at 180°C (350°F) mark 4 for 1½ hours until a fine warmed skewer inserted in the centre comes out clean. Check after 40 minutes and cover with greaseproof paper if overbrowning. Turn out on to a wire rack to cool for 1 hour.

To Freeze
Cool, then overwrap. Freeze for up to 4 months.

To Thaw and Serve
Thaw, wrapped, at cool room temperature.

INDEX